Overview

"Rocky's Rumble Timeline" is a comprehensive book that delves into the life and boxing career of the legendary Rocky Marciano. This book provides a detailed overview of Rocky's journey from his early life and amateur career to becoming the heavyweight champion of the world. With a focus on his fights, training regimen, and impact on popular culture, this book offers a comprehensive look at the life and legacy of one of boxing's greatest icons. In the first chapters, the book introduces readers to Rocky Marciano, providing insights into his childhood, family background, and his introduction to the world of boxing. It explores his amateur career and the transition to professional boxing, setting the stage for the challenges and victories that lay ahead. As the book progresses, it takes readers through the first fights of Rocky's career, highlighting his debut fight, early professional fights, and the building of his reputation. It then delves into the road to the title, showcasing the notable opponents he faced, impressive knockouts, and the stepping stones that led him to the championship fight. Once Rocky becomes the heavyweight champion, the book explores his reign and the challenges he faced in defending the title. It delves into his boxing style, techniques, and the impact he had on the boxing world. The book also covers his retirement decision, life after boxing, and his influence on future boxers. Additionally, the book provides an analysis of Rocky's fights, discussing his fight strategies, strengths, weaknesses, and notable moments. It also addresses controversies and criticisms surrounding his boxing style, controversial fights, and allegations of steroid use. In conclusion, "Rocky's Rumble Timeline" offers a comprehensive and in-depth exploration of Rocky Marciano's life and boxing career. From his early life and amateur career to his reign as the heavyweight champion, this book provides a detailed account of his fights, training regimen, and impact on popular culture. Whether you're a boxing enthusiast or simply interested in the life of a sports icon, this book is a must-read.

Table Of Contents

1 Introduction

1.1 About Rocky Marciano

Rocky Marciano, born Rocco Francis Marchegiano on September 1, 1923, in Brockton, Massachusetts, was an American professional boxer who became one of the greatest heavyweight champions in boxing history. Known for his relentless fighting style, incredible punching power, and indomitable spirit, Marciano left an indelible mark on the sport.

Growing up in a working-class Italian-American family, Marciano faced his fair share of challenges. His parents, Pierino Marchegiano and Pasqualina Picciuto, were hardworking immigrants who instilled in him the values of determination, discipline, and perseverance. Despite his humble beginnings, Marciano's passion for boxing would propel him to greatness.

1.1.1 Early Life and Family Background

Rocky Marciano was the second oldest of six children. His father worked in a shoe factory, and his mother took care of the household. Marciano's parents, both of whom were immigrants from Italy, emphasized the importance of education and hard work. However, Marciano's interest in boxing began to overshadow his academic pursuits.

1.1.2 Introduction to Boxing

Marciano's introduction to boxing came during his teenage years. He joined the local boxing gym, where he quickly caught the attention of his trainers with his raw talent and unwavering determination. Under the guidance of his trainers, Marciano honed his skills and developed a unique fighting style that would later become his trademark.

1.1.3 Rocky's Amateur Boxing Career

Marciano's amateur boxing career was marked by numerous victories and an impressive record. He won the Amateur Athletic Union (AAU) heavyweight championship in 1948, which served as a stepping stone to his professional career. Marciano's amateur success showcased his potential and set the stage for his future accomplishments in the ring.

1.1.4 Transition to Professional Boxing

In 1947, Marciano made the decision to turn professional. He began his journey in the world of professional boxing with a series of fights against various opponents. Marciano's relentless work ethic and determination propelled him to success, and he quickly gained a reputation as a formidable fighter.

As Marciano's professional career progressed, he faced increasingly challenging opponents. His relentless training regimen and unwavering dedication to his craft allowed him to overcome these obstacles and emerge victorious. Marciano's rise through the ranks of professional boxing was a testament to his skill, determination, and unwavering spirit.

Throughout his career, Marciano's fighting style captivated audiences. He was known for his relentless aggression, powerful punches, and ability to absorb punishment. Marciano's fights were often thrilling and action-packed, leaving spectators on the edge of their seats.

In the next chapter, we will delve deeper into the early life and amateur career of Rocky Marciano. We will explore his childhood, family background, and the pivotal moments that shaped his journey towards becoming one of the greatest heavyweight champions in boxing history.

1.2 Purpose of the Book

The purpose of this book, “Rocky’s Rumble Timeline,” is to provide a comprehensive and detailed account of the boxing career of Rocky Marciano, one of the greatest heavyweight champions in history. Through this book, readers will gain a deeper understanding of Rocky’s journey from his early life and amateur career to his reign as the undefeated heavyweight champion and his lasting impact on the sport of boxing.

The book aims to shed light on the various aspects of Rocky’s life, both inside and outside the ring, and explore the factors that contributed to his success. By delving into his upbringing, family background, and introduction to boxing, readers will gain insight into the formative years that shaped Rocky’s character and determination.

Furthermore, the book will provide an in-depth analysis of Rocky’s fights, examining his fight strategies, strengths, weaknesses, and notable moments in the ring. It will explore the impact of his boxing style and techniques on the sport, as well as his influence on future boxers.

Another important aspect of this book is to explore the controversies and criticisms surrounding Rocky’s career. By addressing the criticisms of his boxing style, controversial fights, and allegations of steroid use, the book aims to present a balanced perspective and provide a platform for rebuttal and defense.

Additionally, the book will delve into Rocky’s training regimen, including his physical conditioning, mental preparation, diet, and training techniques. By understanding the dedication and discipline that went into his training, readers will gain a deeper appreciation for the hard work and sacrifice that contributed to his success.

Furthermore, this book will explore Rocky’s impact on popular culture, including his portrayal in movies, documentaries, books, and his influence on music and art. It will also delve into the creation of the iconic character Rocky Balboa and the enduring legacy of the Rocky franchise.

Ultimately, "Rocky's Rumble Timeline" aims to provide readers with a comprehensive and engaging account of Rocky Marciano's boxing career, his impact on the sport, and his lasting legacy. By examining his life, fights, training regimen, controversies, and cultural influence, this book seeks to honor the remarkable achievements of a true boxing legend and inspire readers with his story of determination, resilience, and triumph.

1.3 Overview of Rocky's Boxing Career

Rocky Marciano's boxing career is one that is filled with determination, resilience, and an unwavering commitment to excellence. From his humble beginnings as an amateur boxer to becoming the undefeated heavyweight champion of the world, Marciano's journey is a testament to the power of hard work and dedication.

Born on September 1, 1923, in Brockton, Massachusetts, Rocco Francis Marchegiano, later known as Rocky Marciano, discovered his passion for boxing at a young age. Growing up in a working-class Italian-American family, Marciano faced his fair share of challenges, but his love for the sport propelled him forward.

1.3.1 Early Amateur Career

Marciano's boxing journey began in his teenage years when he joined the local boxing gym. Under the guidance of his trainer, Allie Colombo, Marciano honed his skills and quickly made a name for himself in the amateur boxing circuit. His relentless work ethic and natural talent caught the attention of many, and he soon became a force to be reckoned with.

During his amateur career, Marciano competed in over 50 fights, winning an impressive 49 of them by knockout. His powerful punches and relentless aggression in the ring earned him the nickname "The Brockton Blockbuster." Marciano's amateur success laid the foundation for his future as a professional boxer.

1.3.2 Transition to Professional Boxing

In 1947, Marciano made the decision to turn professional, leaving behind his amateur career and setting his sights on the world of professional boxing. He made his professional debut on March 17, 1947, against Lee Epperson, whom he defeated by a third-round knockout. This victory marked the beginning of a remarkable journey that would see Marciano rise through the ranks and become one of the greatest heavyweight boxers of all time.

1.3.3 The Early Professional Fights

In the early stages of his professional career, Marciano faced a series of opponents who tested his skills and determination. He fought against a mix of experienced fighters and up-and-coming prospects, steadily building his reputation as a formidable force in the ring.

Marciano's early professional fights showcased his relentless style and devastating punching power. He quickly gained a reputation for his ability to knock out opponents with his signature right hand, which became known as the "Suzie Q." His aggressive style and unwavering determination to win endeared him to boxing fans around the world.

1.3.4 The Road to the Title

As Marciano continued to dominate his opponents, his path to the heavyweight title became clearer. He faced a series of notable opponents who posed significant challenges, but Marciano's determination and unwavering focus propelled him forward.

In 1952, Marciano faced his first major test when he fought against former heavyweight champion Joe Louis. The fight ended in an eighth-round knockout victory for Marciano, solidifying his status as a top contender in the division. This victory paved the way for a title shot against reigning champion Jersey Joe Walcott.

On September 23, 1952, Marciano faced Walcott in a highly anticipated bout for the heavyweight championship. In a stunning display of power and resilience, Marciano knocked out Walcott in the 13th round, becoming the new heavyweight champion of the world.

1.3.5 Reign as the Heavyweight Champion

Marciano's reign as the heavyweight champion was nothing short of extraordinary. He successfully defended his title six times, facing off against some of the most formidable opponents of his era. Marciano's fights were characterized by his relentless pressure, powerful punches, and unwavering determination to win.

One of the most memorable fights of Marciano's career took place on September 21, 1955, when he faced off against Archie Moore. Moore, a highly skilled and experienced fighter, proved to be a formidable opponent. However, Marciano's relentless aggression and powerful punches ultimately led to a ninth-round knockout victory, solidifying his status as one of the greatest heavyweight champions in history.

1.3.6 Retirement and Legacy

After defending his title for the sixth time against Moore, Marciano made the decision to retire from professional boxing on April 27, 1956, at the age of 32. With an undefeated record of 49 wins, including 43 knockouts, Marciano left an indelible mark on the sport.

Marciano's retirement marked the end of an era in boxing. His legacy as an undefeated heavyweight champion remains unparalleled, and his impact on the sport continues to be felt to this day. Marciano's relentless work ethic, determination, and never-give-up attitude serve as an inspiration to aspiring boxers around the world.

In the next chapters of this book, we will delve deeper into the various aspects of Rocky Marciano's life and career. We will explore his early life and amateur career, his rise to the heavyweight title, his reign as the champion, and the impact he had on the world of boxing. Join us as we uncover the remarkable story of Rocky Marciano, the Brockton Blockbuster.

1.4 Structure of the Book

In this book, "Rocky's Rumble Timeline," we will explore the remarkable life and boxing career of Rocky Marciano, one of the greatest heavyweight boxers of all time. This book aims to provide a comprehensive and detailed account of Rocky's journey from his early life and amateur career to his reign as the undefeated heavyweight champion and his lasting impact on the world of boxing.

To achieve this, the book is divided into twelve chapters, each focusing on a specific aspect of Rocky's life and career. Let's take a closer look at the structure of the book and what each chapter entails:

Chapter 1: Introduction

In this opening chapter, we will provide an overview of the book and introduce the readers to Rocky Marciano, the man behind the legend. We will delve into his background, the purpose of the book, and provide a brief overview of Rocky's boxing career.

Chapter 2: Early Life and Amateur Career

This chapter will take us back to Rocky's childhood and family background, exploring the influences and experiences that shaped him into the fighter he would become. We will also delve into his introduction to boxing and his impressive amateur career, which laid the foundation for his professional success.

Chapter 3: The First Fights

Here, we will explore Rocky's debut fight and his early professional bouts. We will discuss the challenges he faced, the victories he achieved, and how he began building a reputation as a formidable fighter in the boxing world.

Chapter 4: The Road to the Title

In this chapter, we will examine the notable opponents Rocky faced on his journey to the championship. We will highlight his impressive knockouts and the stepping stones that led him to the highly anticipated title fight.

Chapter 5: Reign as the Heavyweight Champion

This chapter will focus on Rocky's reign as the heavyweight champion. We will delve into his successful title defenses, the legendary fights that defined his career, and analyze his unique boxing style and techniques that made him a force to be reckoned with.

Chapter 6: Retirement and Legacy

Here, we will explore Rocky's decision to retire from boxing and the impact it had on his life. We will delve into his life after boxing, his influence on future boxers, and the lasting legacy he left behind.

Chapter 7: Analysis of Rocky's Fights

In this chapter, we will analyze Rocky's fights in detail. We will examine his fight strategies and tactics, identify his strengths and weaknesses, and highlight notable moments that shaped his career. Additionally, we will discuss the impact his fights had on the history of boxing.

Chapter 8: Unfinished Business

Here, we will explore the potential opponents and dream matches that could have taken place if Rocky had not retired. We will discuss the reasons behind his decision to stay out of the ring and delve into speculations and what-if scenarios that have intrigued boxing enthusiasts for years. Furthermore, we will examine the significance of Rocky's undefeated record.

Chapter 9: Rocky Marciano's Training Regimen

This chapter will provide an in-depth look at Rocky's training regimen. We will explore his physical conditioning, mental preparation, diet, and nutrition, as well as the training techniques and routines that contributed to his success in the ring.

Chapter 10: Rocky Marciano's Impact on Popular Culture

Here, we will examine the influence Rocky Marciano had on popular culture. We will discuss the movies and documentaries that have been made about him, the books and biographies that have been written, and his impact on music and art. Additionally, we will explore the creation of the iconic character Rocky Balboa and the enduring Rocky franchise.

Chapter 11: Controversies and Criticisms

In this chapter, we will address the controversies and criticisms surrounding Rocky Marciano. We will discuss the critiques of his boxing style, controversial fights and decisions, as well as allegations of steroid use. Furthermore, we will provide a rebuttal and defense against these criticisms.

Chapter 12: Conclusion

In the final chapter, we will summarize Rocky's boxing career, highlighting the key moments and achievements that defined his legacy. We will explore his lasting impact on the world of boxing and offer final thoughts on his remarkable journey. Additionally, we will express our gratitude in the acknowledgments section and provide a list of references for further reading.

By following this structure, “Rocky’s Rumble Timeline” aims to provide readers with a comprehensive and engaging account of Rocky Marciano’s life, career, and lasting impact on the world of boxing.

2 Early Life and Amateur Career

2.1 Rocky's Childhood and Family Background

Rocky Marciano, born as Rocco Francis Marchegiano, came from humble beginnings in Brockton, Massachusetts. He was born on September 1, 1923, to Pierino Marchegiano and Pasqualina Picciuto, both Italian immigrants. Rocky was the second oldest of six children, growing up in a close-knit family that valued hard work and determination.

2.1.1 Early Life in Brockton

Brockton, also known as the "City of Champions," had a rich boxing history, and it played a significant role in shaping Rocky's future. Growing up in a working-class neighborhood, Rocky experienced the struggles and hardships that came with the Great Depression. His parents worked tirelessly to provide for their family, instilling in Rocky the values of perseverance and resilience.

2.1.2 Influence of Family

Rocky's parents were a significant influence on his life. His father, Pierino, worked in a shoe factory, while his mother, Pasqualina, took care of the household. They both emphasized the importance of education and encouraged their children to pursue their dreams. Despite their limited resources, they supported Rocky's passion for boxing and stood by him throughout his career.

2.1.3 Early Boxing Exposure

Rocky's interest in boxing began at a young age. He was inspired by the stories of legendary fighters like Joe Louis and Jack Dempsey. As a teenager, he would often visit local gyms and watch the boxers train. It was during these visits that Rocky's love for the sport grew, and he started to dream of becoming a professional boxer himself.

2.1.4 Family Support

Rocky's family played a crucial role in supporting his boxing aspirations. His younger brother, Peter, became his first trainer, teaching him the basics of boxing and helping him develop his skills. Rocky's parents, although initially concerned about the dangers of the sport, eventually recognized his talent and supported his decision to pursue a career in boxing.

2.1.5 Challenges and Sacrifices

Growing up, Rocky faced numerous challenges and sacrifices. He had to balance his boxing training with his studies and part-time jobs to contribute to the family's income. Despite the hardships, Rocky remained focused and dedicated to his craft. He understood that success in boxing would not come easy and was willing to put in the hard work required to achieve his goals.

2.1.6 Family Values and Work Ethic

Rocky's family instilled in him a strong work ethic and a sense of discipline. They taught him the importance of perseverance, integrity, and humility. These values became the foundation of Rocky's character and guided him throughout his boxing career. He carried the lessons he learned from his family into the ring, always giving his best and never backing down from a challenge.

2.1.7 The Marciano Legacy

Rocky's family's influence extended beyond his boxing career. They remained a constant source of support and motivation throughout his life. Even after achieving fame and success, Rocky never forgot his roots and the values his family instilled in him. He remained humble and grounded, always appreciating the love and support he received from his family and the Brockton community.

2.1.8 Impact on Rocky's Boxing Career

Rocky's childhood and family background played a significant role in shaping his boxing career. The values of hard work, determination, and resilience that he learned from his family propelled him to become one of the greatest heavyweight champions in history. The support and sacrifices made by his family gave him the strength and motivation to overcome obstacles and achieve his dreams.

In the next chapter, we will explore Rocky's introduction to boxing and how he transitioned from his early life and amateur career to the world of professional boxing.

2.2 Introduction to Boxing

Boxing, often referred to as the "sweet science," is a combat sport that requires skill, strategy, and physical prowess. It is a sport that has captivated audiences for centuries, with its roots dating back to ancient times. In this chapter, we delve into Rocky Marciano's introduction to the world of boxing and how it shaped his remarkable career.

2.2.1 Early Fascination with Boxing

Rocky Marciano's journey into the world of boxing began at a young age. Growing up in Brockton, Massachusetts, he was exposed to the sport through his father, Pierino Marchegiano, who was an avid boxing fan. Pierino would often take Rocky to local boxing matches, igniting a passion within him for the sport.

From an early age, Rocky was captivated by the skill, determination, and bravery displayed by the boxers in the ring. He admired their ability to overcome adversity and push themselves to the limit. This fascination with boxing would ultimately shape his destiny and lead him to become one of the greatest heavyweight champions in history.

2.2.2 The Influence of Local Boxing Gyms

As Rocky grew older, his interest in boxing intensified, and he sought out opportunities to learn and train in the sport. He began frequenting local boxing gyms, where he observed and absorbed the techniques and strategies employed by experienced fighters. These gyms became his second home, providing him with the necessary environment to develop his skills and hone his craft.

Under the guidance of experienced trainers and mentors, Rocky learned the fundamentals of boxing, including footwork, punching techniques, defensive maneuvers, and ring awareness. He quickly displayed a natural talent and an unwavering work ethic, catching the attention of those around him.

2.2.3 Amateur Boxing Career

Rocky's dedication and commitment to the sport led him to pursue an amateur boxing career. He competed in numerous amateur bouts, gaining valuable experience and refining his skills. His relentless training regimen and unwavering determination propelled him to success in the amateur ranks.

During his amateur career, Rocky showcased his exceptional power and relentless aggression, earning him a reputation as a formidable opponent. He quickly became known for his devastating knockout power, often overwhelming his opponents with his relentless attacks.

2.2.4 Transition to Professional Boxing

After a successful amateur career, Rocky made the decision to turn professional. He recognized that the professional ranks would provide him with the opportunity to showcase his skills on a larger stage and compete against the best fighters in the world.

Rocky's transition to professional boxing was met with both excitement and skepticism. Many questioned whether his aggressive style and unorthodox techniques would translate to success in the professional ranks. However, Rocky remained undeterred, confident in his abilities and determined to prove his critics wrong.

In his early professional fights, Rocky faced a series of tough opponents, each presenting unique challenges. These fights served as stepping stones, allowing him to gain valuable experience and refine his skills. Despite facing adversity, Rocky's relentless determination and unwavering work ethic propelled him to victory after victory.

As Rocky's professional career progressed, his reputation as a fearsome knockout artist grew. He became known for his relentless pressure, devastating power, and iron chin. His ability to absorb punishment and deliver devastating blows made him a force to be reckoned with in the ring.

In the next chapter, we will explore Rocky's early professional fights and the challenges he faced on his journey to becoming the heavyweight champion of the world. We will delve into the notable opponents he encountered, the impressive knockouts he delivered, and the stepping stones that led him to the ultimate title fight. Stay tuned as we continue to unravel the remarkable career of Rocky Marciano.

2.3 Rocky's Amateur Boxing Career

Rocky Marciano's journey in the world of boxing began in his amateur career. It was during this time that he honed his skills, developed his fighting style, and laid the foundation for his future success as a professional boxer. This chapter explores the significant moments and experiences that shaped Rocky's amateur boxing career.

2.3.1 Early Beginnings

Rocky Marciano's interest in boxing was sparked during his teenage years. Growing up in Brockton, Massachusetts, he was introduced to the sport by his friends and family. Inspired by the great boxers of the time, Rocky decided to pursue a career in the ring.

At the age of 16, Rocky joined the local boxing club, where he received his initial training. Under the guidance of his coach, Allie Colombo, Rocky quickly displayed his natural talent and determination. His relentless work ethic and unwavering dedication set him apart from his peers.

2.3.2 Amateur Success

Rocky's amateur career was marked by numerous victories and an impressive record. He competed in various local and regional tournaments, showcasing his exceptional skills and raw power. His relentless pursuit of perfection and his unwavering focus on his goals propelled him to great heights.

One of the defining moments of Rocky's amateur career came in 1947 when he won the Amateur Athletic Union (AAU) heavyweight championship. This victory not only solidified his position as one of the top amateur boxers but also caught the attention of boxing enthusiasts and professionals alike.

2.3.3 Olympic Dreams

Rocky's ultimate goal as an amateur boxer was to represent his country in the Olympic Games. In 1948, he had the opportunity to fulfill this dream when he qualified for the United States boxing team for the London Olympics.

Competing in the heavyweight division, Rocky showcased his exceptional skills and determination throughout the tournament. He advanced through the rounds, defeating opponents with his relentless aggression and powerful punches. However, his Olympic journey ended in the semifinals when he lost a close decision to the eventual gold medalist, Ingemar Johansson of Sweden.

Although Rocky fell short of winning an Olympic medal, his performance in the tournament further solidified his reputation as a formidable boxer. His relentless style and unwavering determination caught the attention of boxing promoters, who saw great potential in him.

2.3.4 Lessons Learned

Rocky's amateur career taught him valuable lessons that would shape his future success as a professional boxer. He learned the importance of discipline, hard work, and perseverance. He understood that success in the ring required not only physical strength but also mental fortitude.

During his amateur career, Rocky also developed his signature fighting style. He relied on his exceptional power and relentless aggression to overwhelm his opponents. His relentless pursuit of victory and his ability to absorb punishment set him apart from other boxers.

2.3.5 Transition to the Pros

After a successful amateur career, Rocky made the decision to turn professional. His amateur experience had prepared him for the challenges that awaited him in the world of professional boxing. With an impressive amateur record and a growing reputation, Rocky was ready to take on the next chapter of his boxing journey.

Rocky's transition to the professional ranks was met with great anticipation. Boxing enthusiasts and experts eagerly awaited his debut, curious to see how his amateur success would translate to the professional level. Little did they know that Rocky would go on to become one of the greatest heavyweight champions in history.

In conclusion, Rocky Marciano's amateur career laid the foundation for his future success as a professional boxer. His early beginnings, amateur victories, Olympic aspirations, and the lessons learned during this time shaped him into the relentless and powerful fighter he would become. The transition to the professional ranks marked the beginning of a legendary career that would leave an indelible mark on the world of boxing.

2.4 Transition to Professional Boxing

After a successful amateur boxing career, Rocky Marciano made the decision to transition to the world of professional boxing. This marked a significant turning point in his life, as he embarked on a journey that would ultimately lead him to become one of the greatest heavyweight champions in history.

2.4.1 Making the Decision

The decision to turn professional was not an easy one for Rocky Marciano. He had achieved great success in the amateur ranks, winning the Golden Gloves tournament and earning a reputation as a formidable boxer. However, he knew that if he wanted to make a name for himself in the boxing world, he would have to take the leap into the professional arena.

Rocky's decision was influenced by a number of factors. Firstly, he had a burning desire to prove himself against the best fighters in the world. He knew that the professional ranks would provide him with the opportunity to face tougher opponents and showcase his skills on a larger stage. Additionally, Rocky had dreams of becoming the heavyweight champion of the world, a feat that could only be accomplished in the professional ranks.

2.4.2 The Early Professional Fights

Rocky Marciano's transition to professional boxing was not without its challenges. He faced a steep learning curve as he adjusted to the different style and pace of the professional game. His first professional fight took place on March 17, 1947, against Lee Epperson. Marciano won the fight by a knockout in the third round, setting the stage for what would become an illustrious career.

In the early stages of his professional career, Rocky faced a series of opponents who were carefully selected to help him gain experience and build his record. These fights allowed him to refine his skills and develop his unique fighting style, characterized by relentless aggression and devastating power.

2.4.3 The Road to Prominence

As Rocky Marciano continued to rack up victories in the ring, his reputation began to grow. He quickly gained a reputation as a fearsome puncher, with a knockout percentage that would become the stuff of legends. His relentless work ethic and unwavering determination propelled him forward, as he climbed the ranks of the heavyweight division.

One of the defining moments in Rocky's early professional career came on October 26, 1951, when he faced the highly regarded Joe Louis. Louis, a former heavyweight champion himself, was nearing the end of his career, but he still posed a significant challenge for the up-and-coming Marciano. In a thrilling fight, Rocky emerged victorious, knocking out Louis in the eighth round. This victory solidified his status as a legitimate contender in the heavyweight division.

2.4.4 The Title Shot

After a string of impressive victories, Rocky Marciano finally earned his shot at the heavyweight title. On September 23, 1952, he faced Jersey Joe Walcott for the championship belt. The fight took place at Municipal Stadium in Philadelphia, and it would prove to be a historic night for Marciano.

In a grueling battle that lasted 13 rounds, Rocky Marciano delivered a devastating right hook that sent Walcott crashing to the canvas. With that knockout, Marciano became the new heavyweight champion of the world. The victory was a culmination of years of hard work and dedication, and it marked the beginning of a legendary reign.

Rocky Marciano's transition to professional boxing was a pivotal moment in his life. It was a decision that would shape his future and set him on a path to greatness. Through hard work, determination, and a relentless fighting style, he would go on to become one of the most celebrated and respected champions in the history of boxing.

3 The First Fights

3.1 Rocky's Debut Fight

Rocky Marciano's debut fight marked the beginning of a legendary boxing career that would go down in history. On March 17, 1947, at the age of 24, Rocky stepped into the ring for the first time as a professional boxer. The fight took place at the Valley Arena in Holyoke, Massachusetts, and it was a momentous occasion for both Rocky and his fans.

3.1.1 The Lead-Up to the Fight

Leading up to his debut fight, Rocky had already established himself as a promising amateur boxer. He had a successful amateur career, winning the Amateur Athletic Union (AAU) heavyweight championship in 1946. This victory caught the attention of boxing promoters and fans, who were eager to see what Rocky could do in the professional ranks.

3.1.2 The Opponent

Rocky's debut fight was against Lee Epperson, a journeyman heavyweight boxer with a record of 0 wins and 1 loss. Epperson, although not a formidable opponent, provided Rocky with the opportunity to showcase his skills and make a statement in his first professional bout.

3.1.3 The Fight

As the bell rang, signaling the start of the fight, Rocky wasted no time in asserting his dominance. He came out swinging, displaying the relentless aggression and power that would become his trademark. Epperson, overwhelmed by Rocky's relentless assault, struggled to mount any significant offense.

Rocky's superior conditioning and relentless pressure began to take its toll on Epperson. In the third round, Rocky landed a powerful right hook that sent

Epperson crashing to the canvas. Epperson managed to beat the count, but it was clear that he was outmatched by the young and hungry Rocky Marciano.

With each passing round, Rocky's confidence grew, and his punches became more precise and devastating. In the fifth round, Rocky unleashed a barrage of punches, culminating in a thunderous left hook that sent Epperson sprawling to the canvas for the second time. The referee had seen enough and waved off the fight, declaring Rocky the winner by knockout.

3.1.4 The Aftermath

Rocky's debut fight was a resounding success. He had made a statement to the boxing world that he was a force to be reckoned with. The victory over Epperson showcased Rocky's raw power, relentless aggression, and unwavering determination.

Following his debut, Rocky went on to win his next 15 fights, all by knockout. This impressive streak solidified his reputation as a rising star in the heavyweight division. Rocky's debut fight set the stage for what would become an illustrious career, filled with victories, championships, and a lasting impact on the sport of boxing.

In conclusion, Rocky Marciano's debut fight was a pivotal moment in his boxing career. It showcased his immense talent, power, and determination, setting the stage for the remarkable journey that would follow. Rocky's victory over Lee Epperson marked the beginning of a legendary career that would see him become one of the greatest heavyweight champions of all time.

3.2 Early Professional Fights

After a successful transition from his amateur boxing career to the professional ranks, Rocky Marciano embarked on a journey that would shape his legacy as one of the greatest heavyweight boxers of all time. In this section, we will delve into the early professional fights that paved the way for his rise to prominence.

3.2.1 The Professional Debut

On March 17, 1947, Rocky Marciano made his professional debut against Lee Epperson at the Valley Arena in Holyoke, Massachusetts. Eager to make a statement, Marciano wasted no time in showcasing his power and determination. In the third round, he unleashed a devastating right hook that sent Epperson crashing to the canvas, securing a knockout victory and marking the beginning of his professional career with a resounding triumph.

3.2.2 The Early Challenges

Following his impressive debut, Marciano faced a series of tough opponents who tested his skills and resilience. One notable early challenge came in his fourth professional fight against Ted Lowry on April 24, 1947. Lowry, an experienced heavyweight, proved to be a formidable adversary. However, Marciano's relentless pressure and relentless punching power ultimately overwhelmed Lowry, leading to a second-round knockout victory.

Another significant early challenge for Marciano came in his eighth professional bout against Carmine Vingo on July 14, 1947. Vingo, known for his durability and toughness, provided a stern test for the young Marciano. Despite Vingo's resilience, Marciano's relentless aggression and powerful punches proved too much to handle. In the sixth round, Marciano unleashed a barrage of punches, forcing the referee to step in and stop the fight, securing another knockout victory.

3.2.3 Victories and Building Momentum

As Marciano continued to climb the ranks of the heavyweight division, he faced a string of opponents who were unable to withstand his relentless assault. One such victory came in his 14th professional fight against Harry Bilazarian on November 14, 1947. Bilazarian, a seasoned fighter, was no match for Marciano's power and determination. In the third round, Marciano landed a thunderous right hook that sent Bilazarian crashing to the canvas, securing yet another knockout victory.

Marciano's momentum continued to build as he faced opponents such as Johnny Pretzie, Artie Levine, and Gino Buonvino, all of whom fell victim to his devastating punching power. These victories not only showcased Marciano's ability to finish fights but also solidified his reputation as a rising star in the heavyweight division.

3.2.4 The Battle of the Undefeated

One of the most significant early professional fights in Marciano's career came on October 26, 1951, when he faced Roland La Starza at Madison Square Garden in New York City. Both fighters entered the ring with undefeated records, adding an extra layer of anticipation and excitement to the bout.

The fight proved to be a grueling battle, with both Marciano and La Starza displaying their skills and determination. Marciano's relentless pressure and powerful punches took a toll on La Starza, but the latter showcased his resilience by weathering the storm and delivering some effective counterpunches.

In the eighth round, Marciano unleashed a devastating right hook that sent La Starza to the canvas. Although La Starza managed to beat the count, Marciano continued his assault, forcing the referee to step in and stop the fight in the eleventh round. With this victory, Marciano not only maintained his undefeated record but also solidified his position as a top contender in the heavyweight division.

3.2.5 The Path to Greatness

The early professional fights of Rocky Marciano laid the foundation for his remarkable career. These bouts showcased his relentless aggression, devastating punching power, and unwavering determination. Marciano's ability to overcome challenges and secure victories against tough opponents propelled him towards greatness.

As Marciano continued his journey, he would face even greater challenges and achieve remarkable victories that would cement his status as one of the most iconic figures in boxing history. But it was these early professional fights that set the stage for his rise to prominence and established the indomitable spirit that would define his legacy.

3.3 Challenges and Victories

Rocky Marciano faced numerous challenges throughout his boxing career, but he also achieved remarkable victories that solidified his reputation as one of the greatest heavyweight champions of all time. This section will delve into the challenges Rocky encountered and the victories he secured along the way.

3.3.1 Early Tests

As Rocky Marciano embarked on his professional boxing journey, he faced a series of tough opponents who tested his skills and determination. In his early fights, he encountered opponents with more experience and established records. These bouts served as valuable learning experiences for the young fighter, allowing him to refine his technique and develop his unique style.

Despite facing more experienced opponents, Rocky showcased his relentless work ethic and unwavering determination. He displayed his trademark power and resilience, often overwhelming his adversaries with his relentless aggression and devastating punches. These early victories not only boosted his confidence but also laid the foundation for his future success.

3.3.2 The Battle with Roland La Starza

One of the most significant challenges Rocky Marciano faced early in his career was his rematch with Roland La Starza. The two fighters had previously met in 1950, with Marciano emerging victorious by a close decision. However, La Starza was determined to avenge his loss and prove himself against the rising star.

Their highly anticipated rematch took place on September 24, 1953, at the Polo Grounds in New York City. La Starza proved to be a formidable opponent, utilizing his superior boxing skills and defensive tactics to frustrate Marciano. The fight was a grueling battle, with both fighters exchanging powerful blows throughout the rounds.

Despite the tough challenge, Marciano's relentless pressure and unwavering determination ultimately prevailed. In the eleventh round, he unleashed a devastating right hook that sent La Starza crashing to the canvas, securing a knockout victory. This hard-fought win showcased Marciano's ability to overcome adversity and solidified his position as a top contender in the heavyweight division.

3.3.3 The Legendary Trilogy with Jersey Joe Walcott

One of the defining moments in Rocky Marciano's career was his legendary trilogy with Jersey Joe Walcott. Walcott, an experienced and skilled fighter, was the reigning heavyweight champion when Marciano first challenged him for the title on September 23, 1952.

Their first encounter, held at Municipal Stadium in Philadelphia, was a closely contested battle. Walcott utilized his slick boxing skills and elusive footwork to frustrate Marciano, who struggled to land his trademark power punches. However, in the thirteenth round, Marciano unleashed a thunderous right hook that connected with Walcott's chin, knocking him out cold. This iconic knockout secured Marciano's first world heavyweight title.

Their second bout, which took place on May 15, 1953, at Chicago Stadium, followed a similar pattern. Walcott proved to be a formidable opponent once again, utilizing his defensive skills to frustrate Marciano. However, in the first round, Marciano unleashed a powerful right hand that sent Walcott crashing to the canvas, securing another knockout victory and successfully defending his title.

The third and final fight between Marciano and Walcott occurred on May 15, 1953, at Yankee Stadium in New York City. This fight would go down in history as one of the most dramatic and memorable heavyweight championship fights of all time. Walcott dominated the early rounds, utilizing his superior boxing skills to outmaneuver Marciano. However, in the thirteenth round, Marciano unleashed a devastating right hook that connected with Walcott's chin, knocking him out and securing his place as one of the greatest heavyweight champions in history.

3.3.4 The Battle with Ezzard Charles

Another significant challenge in Rocky Marciano's career came in his second defense of the heavyweight title against Ezzard Charles on June 17, 1954. Charles, a skilled and crafty boxer, presented a unique challenge for Marciano with his defensive skills and counterpunching ability.

The fight, held at Yankee Stadium, proved to be a grueling battle. Charles utilized his superior boxing skills to frustrate Marciano, effectively neutralizing his power punches. Despite facing a tough opponent, Marciano's relentless pressure and determination allowed him to wear down Charles over the course of the fight.

In the eighth round, Marciano unleashed a powerful right hand that fractured Charles' nose, causing blood to pour down his face. The relentless assault continued, with Marciano landing a series of punishing blows that eventually led to a knockout victory in the eighth round. This hard-fought win showcased Marciano's ability to overcome adversity and solidified his status as an unstoppable force in the heavyweight division.

3.3.5 The Battle with Archie Moore

In his final title defense, Rocky Marciano faced the experienced and crafty Archie Moore on September 21, 1955. Moore, a skilled counterpuncher and former light heavyweight champion, presented a unique challenge for Marciano with his defensive skills and ring intelligence.

The fight, held at Yankee Stadium, proved to be a tough battle for Marciano. Moore utilized his superior boxing skills and defensive tactics to frustrate Marciano, effectively neutralizing his power punches. However, Marciano's relentless pressure and unwavering determination allowed him to wear down Moore over the course of the fight.

In the ninth round, Marciano unleashed a powerful right hand that connected with Moore's chin, sending him crashing to the canvas. Despite Moore's valiant efforts to get back on his feet, he was unable to beat the count, resulting in a knockout victory for Marciano. This victory marked the end of Marciano's illustrious career, with a perfect record of 49 wins and no losses.

Rocky Marciano's challenges and victories throughout his career showcased his unwavering determination, relentless work ethic, and devastating punching power. These triumphs solidified his legacy as one of the greatest heavyweight champions in boxing history.

3.4 Building a Reputation

As Rocky Marciano continued his professional boxing career, he began to build a reputation as a formidable and relentless fighter. His determination, work ethic, and knockout power quickly caught the attention of boxing fans and experts alike. In this section, we will explore the fights that played a crucial role in establishing Rocky's reputation as one of the greatest heavyweight boxers of all time.

3.4.1 Early Professional Fights

After a successful transition from amateur to professional boxing, Rocky Marciano embarked on a series of early professional fights that showcased his raw talent and potential. These fights allowed him to gain valuable experience and refine his skills as he climbed the ranks in the heavyweight division.

In his early professional career, Rocky faced opponents of varying skill levels, from journeymen to up-and-coming contenders. Despite the challenges, he displayed his relentless style and knockout power in each bout. His ability to absorb punishment and deliver devastating blows became evident as he accumulated an impressive record of victories.

3.4.2 The Power of Knockouts

One of the key factors that contributed to Rocky Marciano's growing reputation was his incredible knockout power. Throughout his career, he developed a reputation for delivering devastating punches that could end a fight in an instant. His explosive punching power and relentless aggression made him a feared opponent in the ring.

Rocky's knockout victories not only showcased his physical strength but also demonstrated his ability to capitalize on his opponents' weaknesses. He possessed an uncanny ability to find openings and deliver precise, powerful punches that left his opponents dazed and unable to continue. These knockouts not only thrilled the crowds but also solidified his reputation as a force to be reckoned with in the heavyweight division.

3.4.3 Facing Tough Challenges

As Rocky Marciano continued to climb the ranks, he faced increasingly tough challenges that tested his skills and determination. He encountered opponents who were known for their durability, technical prowess, and experience in the ring. These fights provided Rocky with opportunities to prove himself against formidable adversaries and further enhance his reputation.

In these challenging bouts, Rocky showcased his ability to adapt to different fighting styles and adjust his strategy accordingly. He displayed a relentless work rate, constantly pressuring his opponents and wearing them down with his relentless attacks. His unwavering determination and refusal to back down in the face of adversity earned him the respect of both his peers and the boxing community.

3.4.4 Victories Against Notable Opponents

Throughout his career, Rocky Marciano faced and defeated several notable opponents who were considered some of the best in the heavyweight division at the time. These victories played a crucial role in solidifying his reputation as a true champion and further establishing his place in boxing history.

One of the most significant victories in Rocky's career came against Jersey Joe Walcott in their rematch for the heavyweight title. In a thrilling fight, Rocky knocked out Walcott in the first round, becoming the first heavyweight champion to successfully defend his title with a knockout in the opening round. This victory showcased his power and cemented his status as a dominant force in the division.

Another notable victory came against Ezzard Charles, a skilled and experienced boxer who had previously defeated Rocky in their first encounter.

In their rematch, Rocky displayed his determination and resilience, ultimately winning a unanimous decision and reclaiming the heavyweight title. This victory demonstrated his ability to learn from his mistakes and make the necessary adjustments to overcome tough opponents.

These victories against notable opponents not only added to Rocky's growing reputation but also solidified his place in boxing history. His ability to overcome challenges and emerge victorious against top-level competition further enhanced his legacy as one of the greatest heavyweight boxers of all time.

In the next chapter, we will delve into Rocky Marciano's journey towards the ultimate goal of becoming the heavyweight champion of the world. We will explore the notable opponents he faced along the way and the stepping stones that led him to the title fight. Stay tuned as we continue to unravel the remarkable career of Rocky Marciano.

4 The Road to the Title

4.1 Notable Opponents on the Rise

As Rocky Marciano continued his ascent in the world of professional boxing, he faced a series of opponents who would test his skills and determination. These notable opponents played a crucial role in shaping Marciano's career and preparing him for the ultimate challenge of fighting for the heavyweight title. In this section, we will explore some of the key opponents that Rocky faced on his journey to becoming the heavyweight champion of the world.

4.1.1 Joe Louis

One of the most significant opponents that Rocky Marciano faced early in his career was the legendary Joe Louis. Louis, who had held the heavyweight title for over a decade, was nearing the end of his career when he stepped into the ring with the young Marciano. The fight took place on October 26, 1951, and it was a pivotal moment for both fighters.

Marciano, known for his relentless style and powerful punches, faced a formidable challenge in Louis. Despite being past his prime, Louis still possessed incredible skill and experience. The fight went the full eight rounds, with Marciano ultimately emerging victorious by way of a knockout in the eighth round. This victory over a boxing legend like Joe Louis solidified Marciano's reputation as a rising star in the heavyweight division.

4.1.2 Jersey Joe Walcott

Another notable opponent on Rocky Marciano's path to the title was Jersey Joe Walcott. Walcott, a skilled and experienced fighter, was the reigning heavyweight champion when he faced Marciano on September 23, 1952. The fight took place at Municipal Stadium in Philadelphia and would prove to be a defining moment in Marciano's career.

The fight between Marciano and Walcott was a closely contested battle. Walcott utilized his slick boxing skills and elusive footwork to frustrate

Marciano in the early rounds. However, Marciano's relentless pressure and powerful punches eventually took their toll on Walcott. In the 13th round, Marciano unleashed a devastating right hook that knocked Walcott out cold, securing the victory and the heavyweight title for Marciano. This fight showcased Marciano's ability to overcome adversity and his unwavering determination to become the champion.

4.1.3 Ezzard Charles

After winning the heavyweight title, Rocky Marciano faced a rematch with Ezzard Charles, a former heavyweight champion himself. The first fight between Marciano and Charles took place on June 17, 1954, and ended in a unanimous decision victory for Marciano. However, Charles proved to be a formidable opponent and earned the respect of Marciano.

The rematch between Marciano and Charles took place on September 17, 1954, and it was a grueling battle that tested both fighters' endurance and resilience. Charles utilized his superior boxing skills and defensive tactics to frustrate Marciano throughout the fight. However, Marciano's relentless pressure and powerful punches eventually wore down Charles. In the eighth round, Marciano landed a devastating right hand that knocked Charles out, securing another victory for the champion.

4.1.4 Archie Moore

Archie Moore, a highly skilled and experienced fighter, posed a unique challenge for Rocky Marciano. Moore, known for his defensive skills and counter-punching ability, was considered by many to be one of the greatest light heavyweight champions of all time. The fight between Marciano and Moore took place on September 21, 1955, and it would be Marciano's last professional fight.

Marciano faced a tough battle against Moore, who utilized his defensive skills to frustrate the champion. However, Marciano's relentless pressure and powerful punches eventually took their toll on Moore. In the ninth round,

Marciano landed a powerful right hand that knocked Moore out, securing his 49th consecutive victory and retiring as the undefeated heavyweight champion of the world.

These notable opponents on the rise played a crucial role in Rocky Marciano's journey to becoming the heavyweight champion of the world. Each fight tested his skills, determination, and resilience, ultimately shaping him into one of the greatest boxers of all time. Rocky Marciano's victories over these formidable opponents solidified his place in boxing history and set the stage for his legendary reign as the heavyweight champion.

4.2 Impressive Knockouts

Rocky Marciano's boxing career was defined by his incredible knockout power. Throughout his professional career, he delivered numerous impressive knockouts that left his opponents stunned and the boxing world in awe. In this section, we will explore some of the most memorable knockouts of Rocky Marciano's career.

4.2.1 The Power of the Right Hand

One of the most devastating weapons in Rocky Marciano's arsenal was his powerful right hand. Known for its explosive force, Marciano's right hand was responsible for many of his impressive knockouts. His ability to generate tremendous power and accuracy with his punches made him a force to be reckoned with in the ring.

One of the most memorable knockouts of Marciano's career came in his fight against Jersey Joe Walcott on September 23, 1952. In the 13th round of the bout, Marciano unleashed a thunderous right hook that connected with Walcott's chin, sending him crashing to the canvas. The force of the punch was so immense that Walcott was unable to beat the count, resulting in a knockout victory for Marciano and the crowning of a new heavyweight champion.

4.2.2 The Left Hook from Hell

While Marciano's right hand was his most lethal weapon, he also possessed a devastating left hook that could end fights in an instant. His left hook was known for its speed, accuracy, and the sheer power it carried. Marciano's ability to deliver this punch with precision and force made him a formidable opponent for anyone who stepped into the ring with him.

One of the most impressive knockouts of Marciano's career came in his fight against Ezzard Charles on June 17, 1954. In the 8th round of the bout, Marciano unleashed a lightning-fast left hook that caught Charles flush on the jaw. The impact of the punch was so powerful that Charles was knocked out cold, falling to the canvas in a heap. This knockout victory solidified Marciano's status as one of the most feared punchers in boxing history.

4.2.3 The Devastating Uppercut

In addition to his powerful right hand and left hook, Marciano also possessed a devastating uppercut that could devastate his opponents. His ability to generate tremendous power from his legs and hips allowed him to deliver bone-crushing uppercuts that left his opponents reeling.

One of the most memorable knockouts of Marciano's career came in his fight against Archie Moore on September 21, 1955. In the 9th round of the bout, Marciano unleashed a thunderous uppercut that connected with Moore's chin, sending him crashing to the canvas. The force of the punch was so immense that Moore was unable to beat the count, resulting in a knockout victory for Marciano.

4.2.4 The Accumulation of Punishment

While Marciano was known for his one-punch knockout power, he also had the ability to wear down his opponents with a relentless barrage of punches. His relentless pressure and non-stop attack often left his opponents exhausted and vulnerable to his devastating knockout blows.

One of the most impressive knockouts of Marciano's career came in his fight against Roland La Starza on March 24, 1950. In the 11th round of the bout, Marciano unleashed a relentless assault on La Starza, landing a series of powerful punches that left his opponent defenseless. Unable to withstand the punishment, La Starza eventually succumbed to Marciano's onslaught, resulting in a knockout victory for the "Brockton Blockbuster."

Rocky Marciano's impressive knockouts were a testament to his incredible punching power, accuracy, and relentless determination. His ability to deliver devastating blows with both hands made him one of the most feared fighters of his era. Whether it was his thunderous right hand, lightning-fast left hook, bone-crushing uppercut, or relentless barrage of punches, Marciano's knockouts will forever be etched in boxing history.

4.3 Stepping Stones to the Championship

After a series of impressive knockouts and victories, Rocky Marciano was steadily climbing the ranks of the heavyweight division. In this chapter, we will explore the stepping stones that led him to the ultimate goal of becoming the heavyweight champion of the world.

4.3.1 Early Challenges

As Rocky Marciano's professional career gained momentum, he faced a series of challenges that tested his skills and determination. One of his early stepping stones was his fight against Ted Lowry on March 24, 1949. Lowry was a seasoned fighter with a significant reach advantage over Marciano. Despite the odds, Marciano showcased his relentless style and knocked out Lowry in the third round, proving that he was a force to be reckoned with.

Another notable challenge came in the form of Roland LaStarza, a skilled boxer known for his technical abilities. On March 24, 1950, Marciano faced LaStarza in a highly anticipated bout. The fight went the distance, with Marciano winning by a close split decision. This victory solidified Marciano's reputation as a formidable contender in the heavyweight division.

4.3.2 The Battle with Jersey Joe Walcott

One of the most significant stepping stones on Marciano's path to the championship was his fight against Jersey Joe Walcott on September 23, 1952. Walcott was an experienced and respected boxer who held the heavyweight title at the time. The fight took place at Municipal Stadium in Philadelphia, and it would prove to be a defining moment in Marciano's career.

The bout was a back-and-forth battle, with both fighters displaying their skills and determination. Walcott utilized his slick boxing style, while Marciano relied on his relentless pressure and power punches. In the 13th round,

Marciano unleashed a devastating right hook that connected with Walcott's chin, knocking him out cold. This iconic knockout became known as the "Suzie Q" and secured Marciano the heavyweight championship.

4.3.3 Rematches and Defenses

After winning the championship, Marciano faced several rematches and successfully defended his title against formidable opponents. One of the most notable rematches was against Jersey Joe Walcott on May 15, 1953. This time, Marciano left no doubt about his superiority, knocking out Walcott in the first round with a powerful right hand. This victory solidified Marciano's status as the undisputed heavyweight champion.

Marciano's next defense came against Roland LaStarza on September 24, 1953. This rematch was another closely contested fight, with LaStarza showcasing his technical skills. However, Marciano's relentless pressure and power punches proved too much for LaStarza, and he was knocked out in the 11th round. This victory further cemented Marciano's dominance in the heavyweight division.

4.3.4 The Battle with Ezzard Charles

Ezzard Charles, a skilled and crafty boxer, posed a significant challenge to Marciano's reign as the heavyweight champion. On June 17, 1954, Marciano faced Charles in their first encounter. Charles utilized his defensive skills and counterpunching abilities to frustrate Marciano throughout the fight. However, Marciano's relentless pressure and determination allowed him to secure a unanimous decision victory, successfully defending his title.

In their rematch on September 17, 1954, Marciano faced an even tougher challenge from Charles. The fight was a grueling battle, with both fighters exchanging powerful blows. Marciano suffered a cut over his left eye early in the fight, but he continued to press forward. In the eighth round, Marciano unleashed a barrage of punches that sent Charles to the canvas, securing a knockout victory and solidifying his status as the undisputed heavyweight champion.

4.3.5 The Final Defense and Retirement

Marciano's final defense of his heavyweight title came against Archie Moore on September 21, 1955. Moore was a skilled and experienced fighter, known for his devastating punching power. The fight took place at Yankee Stadium in front of a massive crowd. Marciano faced adversity in the second round when he was knocked down by Moore's powerful right hand. However, Marciano showed his resilience and determination by getting up and ultimately knocking out Moore in the ninth round, successfully defending his title for the sixth and final time.

Following his victory over Moore, Marciano made the surprising decision to retire from boxing at the age of 32. With an undefeated record of 49 wins, including 43 knockouts, Marciano left the sport as one of the greatest heavyweight champions in history.

Conclusion

The stepping stones to the championship were crucial moments in Rocky Marciano's career. From his early challenges to his victories over formidable opponents, each fight played a significant role in shaping his legacy. The battles with Jersey Joe Walcott, Roland LaStarza, and Ezzard Charles showcased Marciano's determination, power, and relentless style. These stepping stones ultimately led him to become the undisputed heavyweight champion and solidified his place in boxing history.

4.4 The Title Fight

After a series of impressive victories and building a reputation as a formidable boxer, Rocky Marciano finally had the opportunity to fight for the heavyweight title. This was the moment he had been working towards his entire career, and he was determined to make the most of it.

4.4.1 The Path to the Title

Before we delve into the details of the title fight, let's take a look at the path Rocky Marciano took to get there. After a string of victories against notable opponents, Rocky's reputation as a knockout artist grew. His impressive record of 43 wins, with 39 of them coming by way of knockout, caught the attention of boxing fans and critics alike.

Rocky's journey to the title began with a fight against the highly regarded Rex Layne on July 12, 1951. Layne was a tough opponent, but Rocky's relentless style and powerful punches proved too much for him. Rocky knocked Layne out in the sixth round, further solidifying his reputation as a force to be reckoned with.

Following his victory over Layne, Rocky faced a series of tough opponents, including Harry Matthews, Joe Louis, and Jersey Joe Walcott. These fights showcased Rocky's ability to withstand punishment and deliver devastating blows. His relentless pressure and unyielding determination became his trademark.

4.4.2 The Title Fight: Rocky vs. Jersey Joe Walcott

On September 23, 1952, Rocky Marciano stepped into the ring with the reigning heavyweight champion, Jersey Joe Walcott. The fight took place at Municipal Stadium in Philadelphia, and the atmosphere was electric. Both fighters were at the peak of their careers, and the world eagerly awaited the outcome.

The fight started cautiously, with both fighters sizing each other up. Walcott, known for his slick boxing skills and counterpunching ability, tried to keep Rocky at bay with his jab. However, Rocky's relentless pressure and powerful punches began to take their toll on Walcott.

In the first round, Walcott managed to land a powerful right hook that sent Rocky to the canvas. It was the first time in his professional career that Rocky had been knocked down. But true to his resilient nature, Rocky quickly got back up and continued to press forward.

As the fight progressed, Rocky's relentless aggression and powerful punches began to wear down Walcott. In the thirteenth round, Rocky unleashed a devastating right hook that connected with Walcott's chin, sending him crashing to the canvas. Walcott tried to get up, but the count reached ten, and the referee declared Rocky the winner by knockout.

4.4.3 The Aftermath

Rocky Marciano's victory over Jersey Joe Walcott made him the new heavyweight champion of the world. It was a historic moment in boxing history, as Rocky became the first heavyweight champion with an undefeated record. His relentless style, knockout power, and indomitable spirit had propelled him to the top of the boxing world.

The victory over Walcott marked the beginning of Rocky's reign as the heavyweight champion. Over the next few years, he defended his title against formidable opponents such as Roland La Starza, Ezzard Charles, and Archie Moore. Rocky's reign as champion was characterized by his relentless work ethic, determination, and knockout power.

4.4.4 The Legacy of the Title Fight

The title fight against Jersey Joe Walcott solidified Rocky Marciano's place in boxing history. It showcased his ability to overcome adversity and his unwavering determination to achieve greatness. Rocky's victory not only made him the heavyweight champion but also established him as one of the greatest boxers of all time.

The fight also had a significant impact on the boxing world. Rocky's relentless style and knockout power inspired a new generation of fighters. His undefeated record became a symbol of excellence and a benchmark for future champions to strive for.

In conclusion, the title fight between Rocky Marciano and Jersey Joe Walcott was a defining moment in Rocky's career. It marked the culmination of years of hard work, determination, and sacrifice. Rocky's victory not only made him the heavyweight champion but also solidified his place in boxing history as one of the greatest fighters of all time.

5 Reign as the Heavyweight Champion

5.1 Defending the Title

After winning the heavyweight championship title in 1952, Rocky Marciano faced the daunting task of defending his title against a series of formidable opponents. Marciano's reign as the heavyweight champion was marked by his relentless determination, unwavering work ethic, and unparalleled punching power. In this section, we will delve into the challenges he faced and the victories he achieved while defending his title.

5.1.1 Early Title Defenses

Marciano's first title defense came on September 24, 1952, against Jersey Joe Walcott. The fight took place at Municipal Stadium in Philadelphia, and it proved to be a grueling battle for both fighters. Walcott, a seasoned veteran, gave Marciano a tough challenge, but the champion's relentless pressure and powerful punches ultimately proved too much for his opponent. In the 13th round, Marciano landed a devastating right hook that knocked Walcott out cold, securing his first successful title defense.

Following his victory over Walcott, Marciano faced a series of tough opponents, including Roland La Starza, Ezzard Charles, and Don Cockell. La Starza, a skilled boxer with a solid defense, managed to take Marciano the distance in their first encounter in 1953. However, Marciano showcased his determination and power in the rematch, knocking La Starza out in the 11th round to retain his title.

In 1954, Marciano faced Ezzard Charles, a former heavyweight champion known for his slick boxing skills. Charles proved to be a formidable opponent, utilizing his superior footwork and defensive abilities to frustrate Marciano. However, the champion's relentless pressure and powerful punches eventually wore Charles down. In the 8th round, Marciano unleashed a barrage of punches, forcing the referee to stop the fight and declare him the winner by technical knockout.

5.1.2 Legendary Battles

One of the most memorable title defenses in Marciano's career came against Archie Moore on September 21, 1955. Moore, a crafty veteran and one of the greatest light heavyweight champions of all time, posed a significant threat to Marciano's undefeated record. The fight took place at Yankee Stadium in New York City, and it was a thrilling back-and-forth battle. Moore showcased his defensive skills and counterpunching ability, frustrating Marciano at times. However, the champion's relentless pressure and powerful punches eventually took their toll. In the 9th round, Marciano landed a devastating right hand that sent Moore crashing to the canvas, securing another successful title defense.

Marciano's next title defense came against Don Cockell, a British heavyweight contender, on May 16, 1956. Cockell, known for his solid boxing skills and durability, aimed to dethrone the champion. However, Marciano's relentless aggression and powerful punches overwhelmed Cockell. In the 9th round, Marciano landed a thunderous right hook that knocked Cockell out, securing yet another successful title defense.

5.1.3 The Marciano-Charles Trilogy

Ezzard Charles proved to be one of the toughest challenges for Marciano during his title reign. After their first encounter in 1954, Charles earned a rematch against Marciano in 1956. The fight took place on June 17, 1957, and it was a grueling battle that showcased the resilience and determination of both fighters. Marciano's relentless pressure and powerful punches proved to be the difference once again, as he secured a unanimous decision victory to retain his title.

Their third and final encounter took place on September 17, 1958, in New York City. This time, Marciano's title was not on the line, as he had announced his retirement shortly after their second fight. The bout was an exhibition match, but it still showcased the competitive spirit and skills of both fighters. Marciano emerged victorious once again, winning by unanimous decision.

5.1.4 The Final Title Defense

Rocky Marciano's last title defense came on September 21, 1955, against the British heavyweight contender, Archie Moore. The fight took place at Yankee Stadium in New York City, and it was a highly anticipated showdown between two legendary fighters. Moore, known for his crafty boxing skills and knockout power, posed a significant threat to Marciano's undefeated record.

The fight started cautiously, with both fighters sizing each other up in the early rounds. Moore showcased his defensive skills, making it difficult for Marciano to land clean punches. However, Marciano's relentless pressure and powerful punches eventually began to take their toll on Moore.

In the 9th round, Marciano unleashed a devastating right hand that landed flush on Moore's chin, sending him crashing to the canvas. Moore struggled to get up but failed to beat the referee's count, resulting in a knockout victory for Marciano.

With this victory, Marciano successfully defended his title for the sixth and final time. It was a fitting end to his reign as the heavyweight champion, solidifying his legacy as one of the greatest boxers of all time.

5.2 Legendary Fights

In this section, we will explore some of the legendary fights that Rocky Marciano engaged in during his career. These fights not only showcased his exceptional skills and determination but also left an indelible mark on the history of boxing.

5.2.1 Marciano vs. Joe Louis

One of the most significant fights in Marciano's career came on October 26, 1951, when he faced the legendary Joe Louis. Louis, a former heavyweight champion and one of the greatest boxers of all time, was nearing the end of his career, while Marciano was still relatively unknown. The fight took place at Madison Square Garden in New York City, and it was a pivotal moment for both fighters.

Marciano entered the ring as the underdog, but he showcased his relentless aggression and powerful punches from the opening bell. Louis, past his prime, struggled to keep up with Marciano's relentless onslaught. In the 8th round, Marciano landed a devastating right hand that sent Louis crashing to the canvas. Louis managed to beat the count, but his corner decided to throw in the towel, resulting in a technical knockout victory for Marciano.

The victory over Joe Louis catapulted Marciano into the spotlight and marked a turning point in his career. It was a symbolic passing of the torch from one great champion to another, solidifying Marciano's status as a force to be reckoned with in the heavyweight division.

5.2.2 Marciano vs. Jersey Joe Walcott

Another legendary fight in Marciano's career was his rematch against Jersey Joe Walcott on May 15, 1953. The first encounter between the two fighters had ended in a knockout victory for Marciano, but Walcott had proven to be a formidable opponent. The rematch took place at Chicago Stadium, and it was a highly anticipated showdown.

The fight started cautiously, with both fighters displaying their defensive skills and counterpunching abilities. Walcott, known for his slick boxing style, frustrated Marciano at times with his elusive movement. However, Marciano's relentless pressure and powerful punches eventually wore Walcott down.

In the 1st round, Marciano landed a thunderous right hand that sent Walcott crashing to the canvas. Walcott managed to beat the count, but Marciano wasted no time in finishing the fight. In the 1st round, Marciano unleashed a barrage of punches, forcing the referee to step in and stop the fight. It was a stunning knockout victory for Marciano, solidifying his dominance in the heavyweight division.

5.2.3 Marciano vs. Roland La Starza

Marciano's fights against Roland La Starza showcased his determination and ability to overcome adversity. The first encounter between the two fighters took place on March 24, 1950, and it was a closely contested battle. La Starza, a skilled boxer with a solid defense, managed to take Marciano the distance, becoming the first fighter to do so in Marciano's professional career. Despite La Starza's impressive performance, Marciano was awarded a unanimous decision victory.

The rematch between Marciano and La Starza took place on September 24, 1953. This time, Marciano was determined to leave no doubt about his superiority. The fight was a back-and-forth battle, with both fighters landing significant punches. However, in the 11th round, Marciano unleashed a devastating right hook that knocked La Starza out cold, securing a knockout victory and avenging his earlier struggle against La Starza.

These legendary fights showcased Marciano's exceptional skills, determination, and ability to overcome adversity. They solidified his status as one of the greatest boxers of all time and left an indelible mark on the history of the sport.

5.2 Legendary Fights

Rocky Marciano's reign as the heavyweight champion was marked by a series of legendary fights that solidified his status as one of the greatest boxers of all time. Throughout his career, Marciano faced formidable opponents and showcased his exceptional skills, determination, and unwavering spirit inside the ring. Let's delve into some of the most memorable fights that defined Rocky's legacy.

5.2.1 Marciano vs. Walcott I - The Cinderella Man

On September 23, 1952, Rocky Marciano faced Jersey Joe Walcott for the heavyweight championship title. Walcott, an experienced and skilled boxer, was considered a formidable opponent for the young Marciano. The fight took place at Municipal Stadium in Philadelphia, and it would prove to be a historic night.

In the 13th round, with just 43 seconds remaining, Marciano unleashed a powerful right hook that connected with Walcott's chin, knocking him out cold. This iconic knockout became known as "The Punch," and it secured Marciano's victory, making him the new heavyweight champion of the world. This fight showcased Marciano's incredible punching power and his ability to turn the tide of a match with a single blow.

5.2.2 Marciano vs. Charles I - The Battle of Champions

On June 17, 1954, Rocky Marciano faced Ezzard Charles in a highly anticipated rematch. Charles was the only fighter to have ever defeated Marciano, and this fight was a chance for Rocky to avenge his only loss. The bout took place at Yankee Stadium in New York City, and it would prove to be a grueling battle between two boxing greats.

Marciano's relentless pressure and powerful punches wore down Charles throughout the fight. In the eighth round, Marciano landed a devastating right hand that sent Charles crashing to the canvas. Despite Charles' valiant efforts to get up, he was unable to beat the count, and Marciano emerged victorious, reclaiming his title as the heavyweight champion. This fight showcased Marciano's determination and his ability to overcome adversity to achieve his goals.

5.2.3 Marciano vs. Moore - The Old Warrior

On September 21, 1955, Rocky Marciano faced Archie Moore in what would be his last professional fight. Moore, a seasoned veteran and a skilled boxer, presented a unique challenge for Marciano. The fight took place at Yankee Stadium, and it would prove to be a battle between two warriors.

Marciano faced adversity early in the fight, as Moore's counterpunching style caused him trouble. However, Marciano's relentless pressure and unyielding determination began to wear down Moore. In the ninth round, Marciano landed a powerful right hand that sent Moore to the canvas. Moore managed to get up, but Marciano continued his assault, eventually knocking Moore out in the ninth round. This victory marked Marciano's 49th consecutive win and solidified his undefeated record. It was a fitting end to a remarkable career.

5.2.4 Marciano vs. Louis - The Passing of the Torch

On October 26, 1951, Rocky Marciano faced his idol and former heavyweight champion, Joe Louis. Louis, past his prime and nearing the end of his career, agreed to the fight as a way to pass the torch to the rising star Marciano. The bout took place at Madison Square Garden in New York City, and it was a historic moment for both fighters.

Marciano showed respect for Louis throughout the fight, but he also demonstrated his superior skills and power. In the eighth round, Marciano landed a powerful right hand that sent Louis crashing to the canvas. Louis managed to get up, but Marciano continued his assault, eventually knocking Louis out in the eighth round. This victory marked a passing of the torch from one boxing legend to another and solidified Marciano's place among the greats.

These legendary fights are just a glimpse into the remarkable career of Rocky Marciano. His relentless determination, punching power, and unwavering spirit made him a force to be reckoned with inside the ring. Marciano's legacy as the only undefeated heavyweight champion in boxing history is a testament to his skill, dedication, and indomitable will.

5.3 Rocky's Boxing Style and Techniques

Rocky Marciano was known for his relentless and aggressive boxing style, which made him one of the most feared and respected heavyweight champions in history. His unique combination of power, stamina, and determination allowed him to dominate his opponents and achieve an undefeated record throughout his professional career. In this section, we will explore Rocky's boxing style and the techniques that made him such a formidable fighter.

5.3.1 Aggressiveness and Pressure

Rocky Marciano was a relentless and aggressive fighter who constantly applied pressure on his opponents. He had an unwavering determination to win and would never back down from a fight. Marciano would often move forward, cutting off the ring and forcing his opponents into close-quarters combat. His aggressive style allowed him to wear down his opponents both physically and mentally, as they struggled to keep up with his relentless attacks.

5.3.2 Power Punching

One of the defining characteristics of Rocky Marciano's boxing style was his incredible punching power. Marciano possessed tremendous strength in both his arms and legs, allowing him to generate devastating knockout punches. He had a unique ability to deliver powerful blows from various angles, making it difficult for his opponents to anticipate and defend against his attacks. Marciano's power punches were often delivered with a combination of speed and accuracy, making them even more lethal.

5.3.3 Stamina and Endurance

Another key aspect of Rocky Marciano's boxing style was his exceptional stamina and endurance. He had an incredible work rate and was known for his ability to maintain a high level of intensity throughout the entire fight. Marciano's relentless pressure and constant movement required immense physical fitness, which he possessed in abundance. His stamina allowed him to outlast his opponents and wear them down over the course of the fight.

5.3.4 Footwork and Defense

While Rocky Marciano was primarily known for his aggressive style and power punching, he also had solid footwork and defensive skills. He possessed quick feet and was able to move around the ring with agility, allowing him to cut off angles and trap his opponents. Marciano's footwork also helped him evade punches and minimize the damage inflicted by his opponents. Although not known for his defensive prowess, he had a solid guard and was able to block and slip punches effectively.

5.3.5 Combination Punching

Rocky Marciano was a master of combination punching, often throwing a series of punches in rapid succession. He would start with a powerful jab to set up his combinations, followed by hooks and uppercuts to exploit his opponent's weaknesses. Marciano's ability to seamlessly transition between different punches made it difficult for his opponents to defend against his attacks. His combination punching was a testament to his speed, accuracy, and timing.

5.3.6 Mental Toughness

One of the most underrated aspects of Rocky Marciano's boxing style was his mental toughness. He possessed an unwavering belief in his abilities and an indomitable spirit that allowed him to overcome adversity in the ring. Marciano's mental toughness enabled him to stay focused and composed, even in the face of intense pressure. He had an uncanny ability to absorb punishment and keep coming forward, which often broke the will of his opponents.

5.3.7 Adaptability

Rocky Marciano was a highly adaptable fighter who could adjust his style and tactics based on his opponent's strengths and weaknesses. He had a keen sense of observation and would study his opponents meticulously before stepping into the ring. Marciano would exploit any weaknesses he identified, whether it be a vulnerability to body shots or a susceptibility to a particular punch. His ability to adapt and make necessary adjustments during a fight was a testament to his boxing intelligence.

In conclusion, Rocky Marciano's boxing style and techniques were a perfect blend of aggression, power, stamina, and adaptability. His relentless pressure, power punching, and exceptional stamina allowed him to dominate his opponents. Marciano's footwork, defensive skills, combination punching, mental toughness, and adaptability further enhanced his effectiveness in the ring. It was this unique combination of attributes that made Rocky Marciano one of the greatest heavyweight champions of all time.

5.4 Impact on the Boxing World

Rocky Marciano's impact on the boxing world cannot be overstated. Throughout his career, he not only achieved remarkable success but also left an indelible mark on the sport. From his relentless work ethic to his undefeated record, Marciano's influence continues to resonate with boxing enthusiasts and professionals alike.

5.4.1 Inspiring Future Generations

Marciano's relentless determination and unwavering commitment to his craft have inspired countless aspiring boxers. His work ethic and dedication to training serve as a blueprint for success in the sport. Many fighters have looked to Marciano as a role model, emulating his style and approach to the ring.

His undefeated record, which stands as a testament to his skill and perseverance, has motivated fighters to strive for greatness. Marciano's legacy has instilled a belief in future generations that anything is possible with hard work and dedication.

5.4.2 Popularizing the Knockout

One of the most significant impacts Marciano had on the boxing world was his ability to deliver devastating knockouts. His punching power and relentless aggression made him a feared opponent in the ring. Marciano's knockout victories captivated audiences and brought excitement to the sport.

His ability to finish fights with a single punch made him a fan favorite and helped popularize the knockout as the ultimate display of dominance in boxing. Marciano's knockout victories became legendary, and his reputation as a knockout artist elevated the sport's appeal to a wider audience.

5.4.3 Elevating the Heavyweight Division

Marciano's reign as the heavyweight champion brought a new level of excitement and prestige to the division. His dominance and undefeated record made him a larger-than-life figure in the boxing world. Marciano's fights drew massive crowds and generated significant media attention, elevating the profile of the heavyweight division.

His battles against formidable opponents such as Joe Louis, Jersey Joe Walcott, and Ezzard Charles showcased the heavyweight division's talent and captivated audiences worldwide. Marciano's success and charisma breathed new life into the division, making it one of the most celebrated and revered in the sport.

5.4.4 Impact on Boxing Strategy

Marciano's unique boxing style and techniques had a lasting impact on the sport. Known for his relentless pressure and relentless pursuit of victory, Marciano popularized the "swarm and destroy" approach. He would overwhelm his opponents with a barrage of punches, wearing them down until they succumbed to his relentless assault.

This aggressive style of fighting revolutionized the sport, inspiring future boxers to adopt a similar approach. Marciano's relentless pressure and ability to maintain a high work rate throughout the fight became a hallmark of his style. His influence can be seen in the fighting styles of many boxers who followed in his footsteps.

5.4.5 Cultural Icon

Beyond his impact on the boxing world, Rocky Marciano became a cultural icon. His undefeated record and larger-than-life persona made him a symbol of determination and resilience. Marciano's story resonated with people from all walks of life, inspiring them to overcome obstacles and achieve greatness.

His popularity extended beyond the sport, with movies, documentaries, and books dedicated to his life and career. Marciano's influence on popular culture can be seen in the creation of the iconic "Rocky" film franchise, which captured the imagination of audiences worldwide.

5.4.6 Legacy of Greatness

Rocky Marciano's impact on the boxing world is undeniable. His undefeated record, inspiring work ethic, and relentless fighting style have solidified his place among the greatest boxers of all time. Marciano's legacy continues to inspire and motivate future generations of fighters, reminding them of the power of determination and hard work.

His influence on the sport can be seen in the countless boxers who have emulated his style and approach to the ring. Marciano's impact on the boxing world will forever be remembered as a testament to his greatness and the mark he left on the sport he loved.

6 Retirement and Legacy

6.1 Retirement Decision

After an illustrious career as the undefeated heavyweight champion of the world, Rocky Marciano faced a difficult decision - whether to retire from boxing or continue his dominance in the ring. This chapter explores the factors that influenced Rocky's retirement decision and the impact it had on his life and legacy.

6.1.1 The Toll of Boxing

Throughout his career, Rocky Marciano had endured countless battles inside the squared circle. The physical toll of boxing was evident, with Marciano suffering numerous injuries, including broken hands, cuts, and bruises. As he approached his mid-thirties, the wear and tear on his body became more apparent, and the recovery time between fights lengthened.

6.1.2 Family and Personal Considerations

Rocky Marciano was a devoted family man, and his decision to retire was also influenced by his desire to spend more time with his loved ones. He had a wife and children who had supported him throughout his career, and he wanted to be present in their lives. The grueling training camps and constant travel associated with boxing took a toll on his family life, and retirement offered him the opportunity to prioritize his role as a husband and father.

6.1.3 Financial Security

Another crucial factor in Rocky's retirement decision was his financial security. Despite his success in the ring, Marciano was not immune to the financial challenges faced by many professional athletes. He had earned substantial purses throughout his career, but he recognized the importance of securing his future and ensuring the financial stability of his family. Retirement would allow him to explore other avenues to generate income and safeguard his wealth.

6.1.4 Desire for a New Challenge

Rocky Marciano was known for his relentless pursuit of excellence, both inside and outside the ring. Retirement presented an opportunity for him to explore new challenges and ventures. He had always been interested in business and had a keen entrepreneurial spirit. By stepping away from boxing, he could channel his energy and determination into other endeavors, seeking new avenues for personal growth and success.

6.1.5 Physical Limitations

As Rocky Marciano approached the latter stages of his career, he began to feel the effects of age on his body. The demanding nature of boxing required peak physical condition, and Marciano recognized that he could not maintain his exceptional level of performance indefinitely. He was aware that his reflexes and speed were gradually diminishing, and he did not want to risk tarnishing his legacy by continuing to fight past his prime.

6.1.6 Longevity and Legacy

Retiring at the pinnacle of his career allowed Rocky Marciano to preserve his undefeated record and secure his place in boxing history. He understood the significance of retiring as the undisputed heavyweight champion, leaving a lasting legacy that would be remembered for generations to come. By retiring on his terms, Marciano ensured that his name would forever be associated with greatness and perfection.

6.1.7 The Final Decision

Ultimately, after careful consideration of all these factors, Rocky Marciano made the difficult decision to retire from professional boxing on April 27, 1956, at the age of 32. He announced his retirement in a press conference, expressing his gratitude to the sport that had given him so much and his excitement for the next chapter of his life.

Rocky Marciano's retirement decision was met with mixed reactions from the boxing world. Some were disappointed that they would no longer witness his incredible displays of skill and power, while others respected his choice to leave the sport on top. Regardless of the opinions, there was no denying the impact he had made during his career.

In the years that followed his retirement, Rocky Marciano remained active in various business ventures and continued to be a beloved figure in the boxing community. He became a successful television commentator and made occasional appearances at boxing events. His retirement decision allowed him to transition smoothly into a new phase of his life, where he could enjoy the fruits of his labor and leave an indelible mark on the sport he loved.

Rocky Marciano's retirement decision was a testament to his character and determination. It showcased his ability to make difficult choices and prioritize what truly mattered to him. His legacy as the undefeated heavyweight champion of the world would forever be intertwined with his decision to retire at the height of his career, solidifying his status as one of the greatest boxers of all time.

6.2 Life After Boxing

After retiring from professional boxing, Rocky Marciano embarked on a new chapter in his life. While he had achieved unparalleled success in the ring, he was determined to find fulfillment and purpose beyond the world of boxing. This section explores the various aspects of Rocky's life after hanging up his gloves and the impact he had on the world outside of the squared circle.

6.2.1 Pursuing Business Ventures

With his competitive spirit still burning strong, Rocky Marciano ventured into the business world. He recognized the importance of financial security and sought opportunities to capitalize on his fame and reputation. One of his first business ventures was a partnership with his close friend and former manager, Al Weill. Together, they formed the "Rocky Marciano Enterprises" and focused on promoting boxing matches and managing up-and-coming fighters.

In addition to his involvement in the boxing industry, Rocky also explored other business opportunities. He invested in real estate, including properties in Florida and Massachusetts. He also dabbled in the restaurant business, opening a successful establishment in Miami Beach called "Rocky's Place." The restaurant became a popular spot for locals and tourists alike, attracting patrons with its delicious food and the chance to catch a glimpse of the legendary boxer.

6.2.2 Television and Film Appearances

Rocky Marciano's larger-than-life persona and captivating personality made him a natural fit for the world of entertainment. He made several appearances on television shows, showcasing his charm and wit. Rocky was a guest on popular talk shows, where he shared stories from his boxing career and engaged in lively discussions with hosts and fellow guests.

His popularity also led to opportunities in the film industry. Rocky made cameo appearances in movies, often playing himself or a character inspired by his boxing career. These appearances allowed him to connect with a wider audience and further solidify his status as a cultural icon.

6.2.3 Public Speaking and Motivational Engagements

Recognizing the impact he could have on others, Rocky Marciano embraced public speaking as a means to inspire and motivate people from all walks of life. He traveled across the country, delivering speeches at various events, including corporate conferences, schools, and community gatherings. Rocky's speeches focused on themes such as perseverance, determination, and the importance of setting goals.

His ability to connect with audiences and share his personal experiences resonated with many, leaving a lasting impression on those who had the privilege of hearing him speak. Rocky's words of wisdom and his unwavering belief in the power of hard work and dedication inspired countless individuals to pursue their dreams and overcome obstacles.

6.2.4 Philanthropy and Charitable Work

Throughout his life, Rocky Marciano remained committed to giving back to his community and helping those in need. He established the Rocky Marciano Foundation, a charitable organization dedicated to supporting various causes, including youth development, education, and medical research. The foundation provided scholarships to aspiring athletes, funded educational programs, and contributed to medical advancements.

Rocky also actively participated in charity events and fundraisers, using his celebrity status to raise awareness and generate support for important causes. He visited hospitals, spent time with children battling illnesses, and made generous donations to organizations that aligned with his values.

6.2.5 Personal Life and Family

While Rocky Marciano's professional life kept him busy, he always made time for his family. He married his high school sweetheart, Barbara Cousins, in 1950, and they had two children together, Mary Anne and Rocco Jr. Despite the demands of his career, Rocky prioritized his role as a husband and father, cherishing the moments he spent with his loved ones.

In his retirement, Rocky enjoyed a quieter life, relishing in the simple pleasures that family and friends brought. He often hosted gatherings at his home, where he would cook his favorite Italian dishes and share stories with those closest to him. Rocky's warm and welcoming nature endeared him to those around him, and he remained a beloved figure in his community.

6.2.6 Legacy and Impact

Rocky Marciano's impact extended far beyond the boxing ring. His relentless work ethic, unwavering determination, and humble demeanor inspired generations of athletes and individuals from all walks of life. His legacy as an undefeated heavyweight champion and his contributions to the world of sports continue to be celebrated to this day.

Rocky's life after boxing serves as a testament to his character and the values he held dear. He demonstrated that success in the ring was just the beginning of his journey, and he used his platform to make a positive difference in the lives of others. Rocky Marciano will forever be remembered not only as a boxing legend but also as a compassionate and influential figure who left an indelible mark on the world.

6.3 Rocky's Influence on Future Boxers

Rocky Marciano's impact on the world of boxing cannot be overstated. His relentless work ethic, unwavering determination, and unbeatable record have inspired countless future boxers to strive for greatness. Marciano's influence can be seen in the way modern boxers approach their training, their fighting style, and their mindset inside and outside the ring.

6.3.1 The Marciano Mentality

One of the most significant ways Rocky Marciano has influenced future boxers is through his mentality. Marciano was known for his incredible mental toughness and never-give-up attitude. He believed in pushing himself to the limit and never backing down from a challenge. This mentality has become a cornerstone of many boxers' training and approach to the sport.

Future boxers have learned from Marciano's example that success in the ring is not just about physical strength and skill but also about mental fortitude. They understand the importance of staying focused, maintaining discipline, and never losing sight of their goals. Marciano's legacy has taught them that the mind is just as crucial as the body in achieving victory.

6.3.2 The Rocky Style

Rocky Marciano's unique fighting style has also had a lasting impact on future boxers. Known for his relentless aggression, powerful punches, and relentless pressure, Marciano was a force to be reckoned with in the ring. His style emphasized constant forward movement, overwhelming opponents with a barrage of punches, and never allowing them a moment to breathe.

Many boxers have adopted elements of Marciano's style, incorporating his relentless pressure and powerful punches into their own fighting techniques. They have learned from his ability to wear down opponents and capitalize on their weaknesses. Marciano's style has become synonymous with an aggressive, high-energy approach to boxing, inspiring future fighters to emulate his success.

6.3.3 Training and Conditioning

Rocky Marciano's dedication to physical conditioning and training has set a standard for future boxers. Marciano was known for his grueling training routines, which included long-distance running, weightlifting, and intense sparring sessions. He believed in pushing his body to the limit to build strength, endurance, and resilience.

His commitment to physical fitness has inspired future boxers to prioritize their training and conditioning. They understand the importance of building a strong foundation of strength and stamina to withstand the demands of the sport. Marciano's training techniques and emphasis on physical fitness have become a blueprint for aspiring boxers, guiding them in their pursuit of excellence.

6.3.4 Perseverance and Undefeated Record

Perhaps the most significant influence Rocky Marciano has had on future boxers is his undefeated record. Marciano retired with a perfect record of 49 wins and no losses, a feat that has yet to be matched in the heavyweight division. His ability to maintain an unblemished record throughout his career has become a symbol of excellence and perseverance.

Marciano's undefeated record has shown future boxers that achieving greatness is possible with hard work, dedication, and unwavering determination. It has instilled in them the belief that they too can overcome any obstacle and achieve their goals. Marciano's legacy serves as a constant reminder that with the right mindset and work ethic, anything is possible.

6.3.5 Role Model and Inspiration

Rocky Marciano's character and humility outside the ring have also made him a role model and inspiration for future boxers. Despite his incredible success, Marciano remained humble and grounded, never letting fame or fortune change him. He was known for his respect for the sport, his opponents, and his fans.

Future boxers look up to Marciano not only for his boxing achievements but also for his integrity and sportsmanship. They strive to emulate his humility, work ethic, and dedication to the sport. Marciano's influence extends beyond the ring, serving as a reminder that true greatness is not just about winning fights but also about being a positive role model and ambassador for the sport.

In conclusion, Rocky Marciano's influence on future boxers is immeasurable. His mentality, fighting style, training methods, undefeated record, and character have left an indelible mark on the world of boxing. Marciano's legacy continues to inspire and motivate aspiring boxers to push their limits, overcome challenges, and strive for greatness. His impact on the sport will be felt for generations to come.

6.4 Legacy and Honors

Rocky Marciano's legacy in the world of boxing is undeniable. Throughout his career, he achieved numerous honors and left a lasting impact on the sport. His undefeated record, remarkable knockout power, and relentless work ethic have solidified his place as one of the greatest heavyweight champions of all time. In this section, we will explore the legacy and honors that Rocky Marciano earned during and after his boxing career.

6.4.1 Undefeated Record

One of the most remarkable aspects of Rocky Marciano's career is his undefeated record. Throughout his professional career, he fought in a total of 49 fights and won all of them, with an impressive 43 victories by knockout. This undefeated record is a testament to his exceptional skill, determination, and unwavering commitment to the sport.

Marciano's undefeated record is a feat that has rarely been achieved in the history of boxing. It is a testament to his ability to overcome challenges and emerge victorious in the face of adversity. His relentless pursuit of perfection and his refusal to accept defeat made him a formidable opponent in the ring.

6.4.2 Heavyweight Champion

Rocky Marciano's most significant honor was winning the heavyweight championship of the world. On September 23, 1952, Marciano faced Jersey Joe Walcott for the title. In a stunning display of power and determination, Marciano knocked out Walcott in the 13th round, becoming the new heavyweight champion.

Marciano successfully defended his title six times, defeating notable opponents such as Ezzard Charles and Archie Moore. His reign as the heavyweight champion lasted from 1952 to 1956, making him one of the longest-reigning champions in the history of the sport.

6.4.3 Hall of Fame Induction

In recognition of his outstanding achievements in boxing, Rocky Marciano was inducted into the International Boxing Hall of Fame in 1990. This prestigious honor solidified his place among the greatest boxers of all time. Marciano's induction into the Hall of Fame was a testament to his impact on the sport and his enduring legacy.

6.4.4 Influence on Future Boxers

Rocky Marciano's fighting style and relentless determination have inspired countless boxers who came after him. His aggressive approach, powerful punches, and unwavering work ethic have become a blueprint for success in the sport. Many boxers have cited Marciano as a major influence on their careers, including legends like Muhammad Ali and Mike Tyson.

Marciano's legacy extends beyond his undefeated record and championship titles. His dedication to the sport and his ability to overcome challenges have served as an inspiration for generations of boxers. His impact on the sport can still be felt today, as his fighting style and work ethic continue to shape the way boxers approach the sport.

6.4.5 Cultural Impact

Rocky Marciano's impact extends beyond the world of boxing. His name has become synonymous with determination, resilience, and the pursuit of excellence. Marciano's story has been immortalized in various forms of popular culture, including movies, documentaries, books, and art.

Movies like "Rocky" and its sequels have captivated audiences around the world, showcasing the underdog spirit and determination that Marciano embodied. The character of Rocky Balboa, played by Sylvester Stallone, was inspired by Marciano's story and has become an iconic symbol of perseverance.

Additionally, numerous books and biographies have been written about Marciano, chronicling his life and career. These works have helped to preserve his legacy and introduce new generations to his remarkable story.

6.4.6 Honors and Recognition

In addition to his induction into the International Boxing Hall of Fame, Rocky Marciano has received numerous other honors and recognition for his contributions to the sport. He was named the Fighter of the Year by Ring Magazine in 1952 and 1954. Marciano was also included in the prestigious Ring Magazine's list of the 100 greatest punchers of all time.

Furthermore, Marciano's impact on the sport has been recognized by various boxing organizations and publications. He has been included in lists of the greatest heavyweight boxers of all time and is often mentioned in discussions about the greatest boxers in history.

6.4.7 Philanthropic Work

Outside of the ring, Rocky Marciano was known for his philanthropic efforts. He used his fame and success to give back to his community and support charitable causes. Marciano was actively involved in various charitable organizations and often donated his time and resources to help those in need.

His commitment to making a positive impact on the lives of others further solidifies his legacy as not only a great boxer but also a compassionate and generous individual.

In conclusion, Rocky Marciano's legacy and honors are a testament to his exceptional skill, determination, and impact on the sport of boxing. His undefeated record, heavyweight championship, induction into the Hall of Fame, and cultural influence have secured his place as one of the greatest boxers of all time. Marciano's legacy continues to inspire and influence future generations of boxers, ensuring that his impact on the sport will be felt for years to come.

7 Analysis of Rocky's Fights

7.1 Fight Strategies and Tactics

Rocky Marciano was known for his relentless fighting style and his ability to adapt to different opponents. Throughout his career, he employed various fight strategies and tactics that helped him achieve his remarkable undefeated record. In this section, we will explore some of the key strategies and tactics that Rocky utilized in the ring.

7.1.1 Aggressive Pressure

One of the defining characteristics of Rocky Marciano's fighting style was his relentless aggression and pressure. He would constantly move forward, applying relentless pressure on his opponents, never giving them a chance to breathe or regroup. This strategy allowed him to control the pace of the fight and wear down his opponents both physically and mentally.

Rocky's aggressive pressure was often accompanied by his signature move, the "Rocky Shuffle." This footwork technique involved him shuffling his feet while moving forward, making it difficult for his opponents to anticipate his movements and counter effectively. The Rocky Shuffle also helped him maintain balance and generate power in his punches.

7.1.2 Powerful Punching

Rocky Marciano was renowned for his devastating punching power. He possessed tremendous strength in both his fists, and his punches were known to be bone-crushing. His strategy was to overwhelm his opponents with a barrage of powerful punches, aiming to knock them out or weaken them significantly.

One of Rocky's most effective punches was his right hand, known as the "Suzie Q." He would often throw this punch with tremendous force, targeting his opponent's head or body. The Suzie Q was a key weapon in Rocky's arsenal and played a significant role in many of his victories.

In addition to his powerful punches, Rocky also had excellent timing and accuracy. He would patiently wait for the right moment to strike, often capitalizing on his opponent's mistakes or openings. This combination of power, timing, and accuracy made him a formidable force in the ring.

7.1.3 Iron Chin and Endurance

Rocky Marciano was known for his exceptional durability and endurance. He possessed an iron chin, meaning he could absorb punches without being knocked down or significantly hurt. This allowed him to take risks and engage in close-quarters exchanges with his opponents, knowing that he could withstand their punches.

Rocky's endurance was a result of his rigorous training regimen and mental toughness. He would push himself to the limit during training, focusing on building his stamina and conditioning. This enabled him to maintain a high level of intensity throughout the fight, even in the later rounds when his opponents would often tire.

7.1.4 Defensive Skills

While Rocky Marciano was primarily known for his aggressive style, he also possessed solid defensive skills. He had excellent head movement, footwork, and the ability to slip and dodge punches. Although he preferred to engage in toe-to-toe exchanges, he was not afraid to use his defensive skills when necessary.

Rocky's defensive strategy often involved bobbing and weaving, making it difficult for his opponents to land clean punches. He would also use his footwork to create angles and avoid being trapped in the corner or against the ropes. These defensive tactics allowed him to minimize the damage inflicted by his opponents and counter effectively.

7.1.5 Adaptability and Ring Intelligence

One of Rocky Marciano's greatest strengths was his ability to adapt to different opponents and situations. He possessed excellent ring intelligence, which allowed him to analyze his opponents' strengths and weaknesses quickly. He would then adjust his strategy accordingly to exploit their vulnerabilities.

Rocky's adaptability was evident in his fights against various opponents with different styles. Whether facing a taller boxer with a reach advantage or a skilled counterpuncher, he would make the necessary adjustments to neutralize their strengths and capitalize on their weaknesses. This adaptability played a crucial role in his success throughout his career.

In conclusion, Rocky Marciano's fight strategies and tactics were a combination of relentless aggression, powerful punching, durability, defensive skills, and adaptability. His ability to apply constant pressure, deliver devastating punches, absorb punishment, and adjust his approach to different opponents made him one of the greatest heavyweight champions in boxing history.

7.2 Strengths and Weaknesses

Rocky Marciano was known for his incredible strength and relentless fighting style. Throughout his career, he displayed a number of strengths that made him one of the greatest heavyweight boxers of all time. However, like any athlete, he also had his weaknesses that opponents tried to exploit.

7.2.1 Strengths

7.2.1.1 Power and Knockout Ability

One of Rocky Marciano's greatest strengths was his exceptional punching power. He possessed a devastating right hand that could knock out opponents with a single blow. His knockout record speaks for itself, with 43 of his 49 victories coming by way of knockout. Marciano's power was not just limited to his right hand; he also had a strong left hook that could cause significant damage. His ability to generate power from both hands made him a formidable opponent in the ring.

7.2.1.2 Endurance and Stamina

Marciano's relentless work ethic and dedication to training allowed him to maintain a high level of endurance and stamina throughout his fights. He was known for his relentless pressure and non-stop attacking style, which often wore down his opponents. Marciano's conditioning was second to none, and he was able to maintain a high work rate for the entire duration of his fights. His ability to keep up the intensity and pressure his opponents relentlessly gave him a significant advantage in the ring.

7.2.1.3 Chin and Resilience

Another strength of Rocky Marciano was his iron chin and resilience. He had an incredible ability to absorb punishment and keep moving forward. Marciano was rarely knocked down in his career, and even when he was, he quickly got back up and continued to fight. His ability to take a punch and keep coming forward was a testament to his mental and physical toughness.

This resilience often frustrated his opponents, as they found it difficult to break his spirit and wear him down.

7.2.1.4 Determination and Heart

Marciano's determination and heart were unmatched. He had an unwavering belief in his abilities and an indomitable will to win. Marciano's relentless pursuit of victory, combined with his never-give-up attitude, often allowed him to overcome adversity and secure victory in challenging situations. His mental strength and refusal to back down made him a formidable opponent for anyone who stepped into the ring with him.

7.2.2 Weaknesses

7.2.2.1 Height and Reach Disadvantage

One of the main weaknesses of Rocky Marciano was his height and reach disadvantage. Standing at just 5'10" with a reach of 67 inches, he often found himself facing opponents who had a significant advantage in terms of height and reach. Taller opponents could keep Marciano at bay with their jabs and maintain distance, making it difficult for him to close the gap and land his powerful punches. However, Marciano's ability to work his way inside and fight in close quarters often nullified this disadvantage.

7.2.2.2 Lack of Defensive Skills

Marciano was primarily an offensive fighter and relied heavily on his power and relentless pressure to overwhelm his opponents. This often left him open to counter punches and made him vulnerable to skilled defensive fighters. Marciano's lack of defensive skills, such as head movement and footwork, made it easier for opponents to land clean shots. However, his exceptional chin and resilience often compensated for his defensive shortcomings.

7.2.2.3 Limited Boxing Technique

While Marciano was a fierce and powerful puncher, he had limited boxing technique compared to some of his contemporaries. He relied heavily on his power punches and often neglected finesse and technical aspects of the sport. Marciano's style was straightforward and predictable, which allowed skilled opponents to anticipate his attacks and counter effectively. However, Marciano's relentless pressure and power often overwhelmed opponents before they could fully exploit his technical limitations.

7.2.2.4 Vulnerability to Body Shots

One weakness that opponents occasionally exploited was Marciano's vulnerability to body shots. Due to his aggressive style and tendency to come forward, Marciano left his body exposed to punches. Skilled opponents who targeted his midsection with well-placed body shots were able to slow him down and weaken his relentless attack. However, Marciano's exceptional conditioning and mental toughness often allowed him to withstand these shots and continue to press forward.

Despite these weaknesses, Rocky Marciano's strengths far outweighed his weaknesses, and he was able to achieve remarkable success in his boxing career. His power, endurance, resilience, determination, and heart made him a force to be reckoned with in the ring. Marciano's ability to overcome his limitations and capitalize on his strengths is a testament to his greatness as a boxer.

7.3 Notable Moments in Fights

Throughout his career, Rocky Marciano had many memorable moments in the ring that showcased his skill, determination, and resilience. These moments not only solidified his status as one of the greatest heavyweight boxers of all time but also left a lasting impact on the sport of boxing. In this section, we will explore some of the most notable moments in Rocky's fights.

7.3.1 The Fight Against Jersey Joe Walcott

One of the most significant moments in Rocky Marciano's career came in his fight against Jersey Joe Walcott on September 23, 1952. This fight was for the heavyweight championship of the world, and it proved to be a true test of Rocky's abilities. In the first round, Walcott caught Marciano with a powerful left hook, knocking him down for the first time in his professional career. However, Rocky showed his resilience by getting back up and continuing the fight.

As the fight progressed, Marciano started to find his rhythm and began to land powerful punches on Walcott. In the 13th round, Rocky unleashed a devastating right hook that connected with Walcott's chin, knocking him out cold. This knockout punch became one of the most iconic moments in boxing history and solidified Rocky's reputation as a knockout artist.

7.3.2 The Rematch Against Ezzard Charles

After winning the heavyweight title, Rocky faced Ezzard Charles in a rematch on June 17, 1954. Charles was known for his defensive skills and had previously defeated Marciano in their first encounter. This fight proved to be a grueling battle for both fighters, with Charles using his superior boxing skills to frustrate Rocky.

In the eighth round, Marciano suffered a deep cut above his left eye due to an accidental headbutt. Despite the blood streaming down his face, Rocky refused to let the injury deter him. He continued to press forward, relentlessly attacking Charles with his trademark power punches. In the 14th round, Marciano landed a thunderous right hand that sent Charles crashing to the canvas. This knockout victory showcased Rocky's determination and his ability to overcome adversity.

7.3.3 The Fight Against Archie Moore

On September 21, 1955, Rocky Marciano faced Archie Moore in what would be his last professional fight. Moore was a seasoned veteran and a highly skilled boxer, known for his knockout power. This fight proved to be a true test for Marciano, as Moore was able to avoid many of Rocky's punches with his elusive defense.

In the ninth round, Marciano found an opening and unleashed a devastating right hand that connected with Moore's chin. The punch sent Moore sprawling to the canvas, and he was unable to beat the count. With this knockout victory, Rocky Marciano ended his career with an impressive record of 49 wins, 0 losses, and 43 knockouts. This fight solidified his legacy as the only heavyweight champion to retire undefeated.

7.3.4 The Fight Against Roland La Starza

In their first encounter on March 24, 1950, Rocky Marciano faced Roland La Starza in a closely contested fight. La Starza proved to be a tough opponent, using his boxing skills to frustrate Marciano throughout the match. However, Rocky's relentless pressure and power punches eventually wore down La Starza, leading to a unanimous decision victory for Marciano.

In their rematch on September 24, 1953, Marciano once again faced La Starza. This time, Rocky was determined to make a statement and showcase his dominance. In the 11th round, Marciano landed a powerful right hand that sent La Starza crashing to the canvas. Despite his best efforts, La Starza was unable to beat the count, and Rocky secured another knockout victory.

7.3.5 The Fight Against Joe Louis

On October 26, 1951, Rocky Marciano faced the legendary Joe Louis in what would be Louis' last professional fight. Louis, a former heavyweight champion, was past his prime, but he still possessed formidable skills and punching power. Marciano showed respect for his idol throughout the fight but also displayed his determination to win.

In the eighth round, Marciano landed a powerful right hand that sent Louis sprawling to the canvas. Louis managed to get up, but Rocky continued to press the attack. In the following round, Marciano unleashed a barrage of punches that forced the referee to stop the fight, securing a technical knockout victory for Rocky. This fight marked the passing of the torch from one great champion to another and showcased Marciano's ability to overcome his idols.

These notable moments in Rocky Marciano's fights highlight his incredible skill, determination, and ability to overcome adversity. From his knockout victory over Jersey Joe Walcott to his dominant performances against Ezzard Charles and Archie Moore, Rocky left an indelible mark on the sport of boxing. His legacy as an undefeated heavyweight champion continues to inspire future generations of boxers, and his fights will forever be remembered as some of the most memorable moments in boxing history.

7.4 Impact on Boxing History

Rocky Marciano's impact on boxing history cannot be overstated. His undefeated record, relentless fighting style, and incredible knockout power have solidified his place as one of the greatest heavyweight champions of all time. Throughout his career, Marciano left an indelible mark on the sport, influencing future generations of boxers and shaping the way the game is played.

7.4.1 Changing the Perception of Heavyweight Boxing

Before Rocky Marciano, the heavyweight division was dominated by fighters who relied on size and brute strength. Marciano, however, brought a new level of athleticism and technique to the ring. He showcased the importance of speed, agility, and footwork, proving that a smaller fighter could overcome larger opponents through skill and determination.

Marciano's success challenged the conventional wisdom of heavyweight boxing, inspiring a new generation of fighters to focus on conditioning, strategy, and precision. His relentless work ethic and dedication to training set a new standard for the sport, encouraging fighters to push their limits and strive for greatness.

7.4.2 Popularizing the Knockout

One of the most significant contributions Marciano made to boxing history was his ability to deliver devastating knockouts. Out of his 49 professional victories, 43 came by way of knockout, giving him one of the highest knockout percentages in heavyweight history. Marciano's punching power and relentless aggression captivated audiences and brought excitement back to the heavyweight division.

His knockout victories not only thrilled fans but also inspired future fighters to seek the same explosive finishes. Marciano's ability to end fights with a single punch showcased the potential for a dramatic and decisive conclusion, making knockouts a sought-after outcome in the sport.

7.4.3 The Rocky Marciano Fighting Spirit

Rocky Marciano's fighting spirit and never-give-up attitude have become legendary in the world of boxing. He was known for his incredible stamina, unwavering determination, and ability to come back from adversity. Marciano's relentless pursuit of victory, even in the face of seemingly insurmountable odds, has become a source of inspiration for fighters across generations.

His never-say-die mentality has become synonymous with the sport itself, reminding fighters that anything is possible with hard work, resilience, and a refusal to quit. Marciano's legacy serves as a constant reminder that success in boxing, and in life, often comes down to sheer willpower and the refusal to accept defeat.

7.4.4 Influence on Training and Conditioning

Rocky Marciano's rigorous training regimen and commitment to physical conditioning revolutionized the way boxers prepare for fights. He was known for his grueling workouts, which included long-distance running, weightlifting, and intense sparring sessions. Marciano's dedication to fitness and strength training set a new standard for boxers, emphasizing the importance of being in peak physical condition.

His training techniques and routines have been studied and emulated by countless fighters, with many adopting similar methods to improve their own performance. Marciano's emphasis on endurance, strength, and mental toughness has become a cornerstone of modern boxing training, ensuring that fighters are prepared both physically and mentally for the challenges they will face in the ring.

7.4.5 Inspiring Future Generations

Rocky Marciano's impact extends far beyond his own era. His relentless work ethic, undefeated record, and fighting spirit continue to inspire and motivate boxers to this day. Many fighters have cited Marciano as a role model and a source of inspiration, striving to emulate his success and leave their own mark on the sport.

Marciano's legacy serves as a reminder that greatness can be achieved through hard work, discipline, and a never-give-up attitude. His story resonates with fighters of all backgrounds, reminding them that success is not determined by size or natural talent alone but by the determination and dedication to be the best.

7.4.6 Shaping the Heavyweight Division

Rocky Marciano's reign as the heavyweight champion had a profound impact on the division itself. His dominance and undefeated record brought a level of excitement and prestige back to the heavyweight title. Marciano's fights were highly anticipated events, drawing large crowds and capturing the attention of the world.

His success also paved the way for future generations of heavyweight champions, inspiring them to strive for greatness and leave their own mark on the sport. Marciano's influence can be seen in the fighting styles and approaches of subsequent champions, as they sought to replicate his success and build upon his legacy.

In conclusion, Rocky Marciano's impact on boxing history cannot be overstated. His undefeated record, knockout power, and relentless fighting style changed the perception of heavyweight boxing and inspired future generations of fighters. Marciano's legacy lives on in the training techniques, fighting spirit, and determination of boxers around the world. His influence on the sport will continue to be felt for generations to come.

8 Unfinished Business

8.1 Potential Opponents and Dream Matches

Throughout his career, Rocky Marciano faced numerous formidable opponents and established himself as one of the greatest heavyweight boxers of all time. However, even after retiring with an undefeated record, there were still potential opponents and dream matches that fans and boxing enthusiasts speculated about. Let's explore some of these matchups that could have taken place if Rocky had continued his boxing career.

8.1.1 Joe Louis

Joe Louis, also known as the "Brown Bomber," was one of the most dominant heavyweight champions in boxing history. He held the title for over 11 years and successfully defended it 25 times. Although Louis retired in 1949, there was still speculation about a potential matchup between him and Rocky Marciano. The clash between these two legendary fighters would have been a battle of generations, with Marciano's relentless aggression and power against Louis' technical skills and experience.

8.1.2 Muhammad Ali

Muhammad Ali, formerly known as Cassius Clay, emerged as one of the most iconic figures in sports and transcended the world of boxing. His speed, agility, and unorthodox fighting style made him a formidable opponent for anyone in the ring. Although Ali and Marciano never fought each other, their styles and personalities made this dream matchup a topic of discussion among boxing fans. The clash between Ali's finesse and Marciano's relentless pressure would have undoubtedly been a historic event.

8.1.3 Sonny Liston

Sonny Liston, known for his intimidating presence and devastating knockout power, was a dominant force in the heavyweight division during the 1960s.

Liston's reign as champion was cut short by Muhammad Ali, but before that, there were talks of a potential matchup between Liston and Marciano. Liston's size and power would have posed a significant challenge for Marciano, but his relentless determination and iron chin would have made for an intriguing clash of styles.

8.1.4 George Foreman

George Foreman, known for his incredible punching power, became the heavyweight champion in 1973 by defeating Joe Frazier. Foreman's aggressive style and knockout ability made him a feared opponent in the ring. If Marciano had continued his career into the 1970s, a matchup between him and Foreman would have been a clash of two powerhouses. Marciano's relentless pressure and durability against Foreman's devastating punches would have made for an explosive encounter.

8.1.5 Larry Holmes

Larry Holmes, who held the heavyweight title from 1978 to 1985, was known for his exceptional jab and boxing skills. Holmes successfully defended his title 20 times, establishing himself as one of the most dominant champions of his era. If Marciano had come out of retirement to face Holmes, it would have been a battle between two fighters with contrasting styles. Marciano's aggressive pressure against Holmes' technical prowess would have made for an intriguing matchup.

8.1.6 Mike Tyson

Mike Tyson, known for his ferocious power and explosive knockouts, became the youngest heavyweight champion in history at the age of 20. His aggressive style and devastating punches made him a force to be reckoned with in the ring. If Marciano had faced Tyson during his prime, it would have been a battle between two fighters with immense power. Marciano's relentless pressure against Tyson's explosive punches would have made for an electrifying matchup.

8.1.7 Evander Holyfield

Evander Holyfield, a multiple-time heavyweight champion, was known for his heart, determination, and ability to adapt to different styles. Holyfield's boxing skills and resilience made him a formidable opponent for anyone he faced. If Marciano had come out of retirement to face Holyfield, it would have been a clash between two fighters with unwavering determination. Marciano's relentless pressure against Holyfield's technical skills and heart would have made for an epic showdown.

8.1.8 Lennox Lewis

Lennox Lewis, a dominant heavyweight champion in the 1990s and early 2000s, possessed a unique combination of size, power, and boxing skills. Lewis successfully defended his title against numerous top contenders during his reign. If Marciano had faced Lewis, it would have been a battle between two fighters with contrasting styles. Marciano's relentless pressure against Lewis' technical abilities and size would have made for an intriguing matchup.

While these potential opponents and dream matches never materialized, the speculation surrounding them showcases the enduring legacy of Rocky Marciano. His undefeated record and relentless fighting style continue to captivate the imagination of boxing fans and historians alike. Rocky's impact on the sport of boxing remains unparalleled, and his name will forever be associated with greatness.

8.2 Reasons for Not Returning to the Ring

Throughout his career, Rocky Marciano displayed an unwavering dedication to the sport of boxing. His relentless work ethic, indomitable spirit, and unmatched determination propelled him to become one of the greatest heavyweight champions of all time. However, despite his undeniable success and the allure of potential dream matches and lucrative opportunities, Marciano made the decision to retire at the peak of his career. This section explores the reasons behind his choice and sheds light on the factors that influenced his decision.

8.2.1 Satisfaction with Accomplishments

One of the primary reasons for Rocky Marciano's retirement was his deep sense of satisfaction with his accomplishments in the ring. By the time he retired, Marciano had achieved an unprecedented record of 49 wins, with 43 of them coming by way of knockout. He had successfully defended his heavyweight title six times, defeating some of the most formidable opponents of his era. Marciano had proven himself as the undisputed champion, and he felt that he had nothing left to prove to himself or to the boxing world.

8.2.2 Desire for a Normal Life

Another significant factor that influenced Marciano's decision to retire was his desire for a normal life outside of boxing. Throughout his career, he had dedicated himself entirely to the sport, sacrificing time with his family and personal pursuits. Marciano longed for a life beyond the ring, where he could spend quality time with his loved ones and pursue other interests. He wanted to enjoy the simple pleasures of life and escape the constant physical and mental demands of professional boxing.

8.2.3 Concerns for Health and Well-being

As a boxer, Marciano was well aware of the physical toll that the sport took on his body. He had endured countless grueling training sessions and intense fights, which inevitably led to injuries and wear and tear. Marciano recognized the potential long-term consequences of continuing to compete in the ring, both physically and mentally. He wanted to preserve his health and well-being, prioritizing a future free from the potential complications that often plagued retired boxers.

8.2.4 Family and Personal Priorities

Family played a significant role in Marciano's decision to retire. He cherished his wife, Barbara, and their children, and he wanted to be present in their lives. Marciano understood the sacrifices his family had made throughout his career, and he wanted to repay their unwavering support and love by being there for them. Retirement allowed him to focus on his family and create lasting memories with them, something that would have been challenging to achieve had he continued to compete.

8.2.5 Financial Security

Despite the allure of potential big-money fights, Marciano's decision to retire was not influenced by financial considerations. He had amassed a considerable fortune during his career, and he was financially secure. Marciano was not driven by the need for more wealth or fame but rather by the desire for personal fulfillment and a sense of contentment.

8.2.6 Maintaining an Undefeated Record

One of the defining aspects of Rocky Marciano's career was his undefeated record. He retired as the only heavyweight champion to retire without a single loss. Marciano understood the significance of this achievement and the impact it would have on his legacy. By retiring undefeated, he solidified his place in boxing history and ensured that his name would forever be associated with greatness. Returning to the ring would have risked tarnishing his perfect record, and Marciano was unwilling to take that chance.

8.2.7 Longevity and Preservation of Legacy

Marciano was acutely aware of the toll that age and time could take on a boxer's skills and abilities. He recognized that his physical prime would not last forever and that his reflexes and speed would inevitably decline with age. By retiring at the age of 32, Marciano preserved his legacy as an undefeated champion and avoided the potential decline that often accompanies aging fighters. He wanted to be remembered as the dominant force he was during his career, rather than a shadow of his former self.

8.2.8 Contentment with Life After Boxing

After retiring from boxing, Marciano found fulfillment in various endeavors. He pursued a career in broadcasting, becoming a successful sports commentator and analyst. He also ventured into business, investing in real estate and other ventures. Marciano enjoyed a fulfilling life outside of the ring, surrounded by his loved ones and engaging in activities that brought him joy and satisfaction. He had successfully transitioned into a new chapter of his life, one that allowed him to explore different passions and make a positive impact beyond the realm of boxing.

In conclusion, Rocky Marciano's decision to retire from boxing was influenced by a combination of factors. His satisfaction with his accomplishments, desire for a normal life, concerns for his health and well-being, family and personal priorities, financial security, the desire to maintain an undefeated record, the preservation of his legacy, and contentment with life after boxing all played a role in shaping his decision. Marciano's retirement allowed him to leave the sport on his own terms, cementing his status as one of the greatest boxers of all time and ensuring that his legacy would endure for generations to come.

8.3 Speculations and What-If Scenarios

Throughout Rocky Marciano's career, there were several speculations and what-if scenarios that intrigued fans and boxing enthusiasts. These hypothetical situations often revolved around potential opponents that Marciano never faced or dream matches that could have taken place. While these scenarios can never be definitively answered, they provide an interesting glimpse into the possibilities that could have unfolded in Rocky's boxing journey.

8.3.1 Dream Matches

One of the most intriguing what-if scenarios in Rocky Marciano's career is the possibility of him facing other legendary heavyweight champions. Fans and experts often speculate about how Marciano would have fared against fighters like Muhammad Ali, Joe Louis, or Mike Tyson. These dream matches would have pitted two boxing greats against each other, each with their unique styles and strengths.

In a hypothetical matchup against Muhammad Ali, Marciano's relentless pressure and power punching would have been tested against Ali's speed, agility, and defensive skills. It would have been a clash of styles, with Marciano's relentless aggression trying to break through Ali's elusive movement and counterpunching. The outcome of this dream match is a subject of much debate among boxing fans.

Another dream match that fans often ponder is a showdown between Rocky Marciano and Joe Louis. Both fighters possessed incredible punching power, and their styles would have made for an explosive encounter. Marciano's relentless pressure and iron chin against Louis' technical skills and devastating knockout ability would have made for an unforgettable fight.

The idea of a matchup between Rocky Marciano and Mike Tyson also captures the imagination of boxing fans. Both fighters were known for their knockout power and aggressive fighting styles. Marciano's relentless pressure and durability against Tyson's explosive punching and intimidating presence would have been a clash of titans.

8.3.2 Unfinished Business

While Rocky Marciano retired as the undefeated heavyweight champion, there were a few potential opponents that he never faced. One notable name that often comes up in discussions is Floyd Patterson. Patterson, who later became a heavyweight champion himself, was an up-and-coming fighter during Marciano's reign. Many fans wonder how a matchup between the two would have played out, considering their contrasting styles and skill sets.

Another potential opponent that Marciano never faced was Sonny Liston. Liston, known for his immense power and intimidating presence, was a dominant force in the heavyweight division after Marciano's retirement. A fight between Marciano and Liston would have been a clash of generations, with Marciano's relentless pressure against Liston's devastating punching power.

8.3.3 Legacy of Undefeated Record

Rocky Marciano's undefeated record of 49-0 is a remarkable achievement that has stood the test of time. However, there are speculations about how long Marciano could have continued his winning streak if he had chosen to fight beyond his retirement in 1956. Many wonder if he could have surpassed the 50-win mark or even gone on to achieve an unprecedented 60-0 record.

Considering Marciano's relentless work ethic, determination, and indomitable spirit, it is not far-fetched to imagine him continuing his winning ways. However, the heavyweight division is known for its unpredictability, and there were several formidable opponents on the horizon during that era. Speculating on the outcome of these hypothetical matchups is purely conjecture, but it is undeniable that Marciano's legacy would have been further solidified with additional victories.

8.3.4 The Marciano Era

Rocky Marciano's era in boxing was marked by his dominance and undefeated record. Speculating on what could have happened during his career is a fascinating exercise that showcases the impact he had on the sport. While we can only imagine the outcomes of dream matches and potential opponents, it is clear that Marciano's legacy as one of the greatest heavyweight champions of all time remains intact.

The what-if scenarios surrounding Rocky Marciano's career add to the mystique and intrigue of his boxing journey. They allow fans to engage in discussions and debates, imagining the possibilities that could have unfolded in the ring. Ultimately, however, it is the accomplishments and legacy that Marciano left behind that define his place in boxing history.

8.4 Legacy of Undefeated Record

Rocky Marciano's undefeated record is one of the most remarkable achievements in the history of boxing. Throughout his career, Marciano displayed an unwavering determination and an indomitable spirit that allowed him to overcome any challenge in the ring. His legacy as the only heavyweight champion to retire undefeated is a testament to his skill, resilience, and sheer willpower.

8.4.1 The Undefeated Record

Rocky Marciano's professional boxing career spanned from 1947 to 1955, during which he fought a total of 49 fights, winning all of them. This incredible feat is unparalleled in the heavyweight division and solidifies his place as one of the greatest boxers of all time. Marciano's undefeated record is a testament to his exceptional talent, work ethic, and relentless pursuit of perfection.

8.4.2 The Importance of an Undefeated Record

An undefeated record holds immense significance in the world of boxing. It signifies a boxer's ability to consistently overcome formidable opponents and emerge victorious. It showcases their skill, resilience, and ability to adapt to different styles and strategies. For Rocky Marciano, his undefeated record not only solidified his place in boxing history but also elevated him to legendary status.

8.4.3 The Pressure of an Undefeated Record

Maintaining an undefeated record can be an immense burden for any boxer. The pressure to continue winning and the fear of tarnishing a perfect record can weigh heavily on a fighter's mind. However, Rocky Marciano embraced this pressure and used it as motivation to push himself to new heights. He understood the significance of his undefeated record and was determined to protect it at all costs.

8.4.4 The Challenges Faced

Throughout his career, Rocky Marciano faced numerous challenges that tested his undefeated record. He fought against some of the toughest opponents in the heavyweight division, including Joe Louis, Jersey Joe Walcott, and Ezzard Charles. These fighters were renowned for their skill, power, and experience, but Marciano's relentless determination and unwavering focus allowed him to overcome each challenge and emerge victorious.

8.4.5 The Impact on Boxing History

Rocky Marciano's undefeated record had a profound impact on the sport of boxing. It inspired future generations of fighters to strive for perfection and to believe in their abilities. Marciano's relentless pursuit of victory and his refusal to accept defeat became a source of inspiration for aspiring boxers around the world. His legacy continues to shape the sport to this day.

8.4.6 The Enduring Legacy

Rocky Marciano's undefeated record is a testament to his skill, determination, and unwavering commitment to excellence. It serves as a reminder that with hard work, dedication, and a never-give-up attitude, anything is possible. Marciano's legacy as the only heavyweight champion to retire undefeated will forever be etched in the annals of boxing history, and his name will always be synonymous with greatness.

8.4.7 The Inspiration for Future Generations

Rocky Marciano's undefeated record continues to inspire and motivate future generations of boxers. His story serves as a reminder that success is not achieved overnight but through years of hard work, sacrifice, and perseverance. Marciano's legacy encourages young fighters to believe in themselves, to embrace challenges, and to never back down in the face of adversity.

8.4.8 The Unbreakable Record

Rocky Marciano's undefeated record remains unbroken to this day. Many great boxers have come and gone, but none have been able to replicate Marciano's remarkable achievement. As the years go by, his record becomes even more impressive, solidifying his place as one of the greatest boxers of all time. Marciano's undefeated record stands as a testament to his unparalleled skill, determination, and legacy in the sport of boxing.

8.4.9 The Lasting Impact

Rocky Marciano's undefeated record continues to captivate the imagination of boxing fans and experts alike. It serves as a constant reminder of the heights that can be achieved through hard work, dedication, and an unwavering belief in oneself. Marciano's legacy will forever be etched in the history of boxing, and his undefeated record will continue to inspire future generations of fighters to strive for greatness.

9 Rocky Marciano's Training Regimen

9.1 Physical Conditioning

Physical conditioning played a crucial role in Rocky Marciano's success as a boxer. Known for his relentless work ethic and dedication to training, Marciano pushed himself to the limits to ensure he was in peak physical condition for every fight. His training regimen consisted of a combination of strength training, cardiovascular exercises, and specific boxing drills designed to enhance his power, speed, and endurance.

9.1.1 Strength Training

Marciano understood the importance of building strength to deliver powerful punches and withstand the physical demands of boxing. He incorporated weightlifting into his training routine, focusing on exercises that targeted his upper body, core, and legs. Marciano would perform exercises such as bench presses, squats, deadlifts, and overhead presses to develop overall strength and explosive power.

To further enhance his punching power, Marciano also utilized resistance training techniques. He would attach weights to his wrists and ankles while shadowboxing or hitting the heavy bag, forcing his muscles to work harder and increasing the intensity of his punches. This method helped him develop the devastating knockout power that became his trademark in the ring.

9.1.2 Cardiovascular Conditioning

Endurance was another crucial aspect of Marciano's physical conditioning. He recognized the importance of maintaining a high level of cardiovascular fitness to sustain his relentless fighting style throughout the duration of a fight. Marciano would engage in various cardiovascular exercises such as running, skipping rope, and cycling to improve his stamina and lung capacity.

Long-distance running was a fundamental part of Marciano's training routine. He would often run several miles each day, focusing on building both aerobic and anaerobic endurance. This type of training allowed him to maintain a high work rate during fights and outlast his opponents in the later rounds.

Skipping rope was another staple of Marciano's training regimen. Not only did it improve his footwork and coordination, but it also provided an intense cardiovascular workout. Marciano would spend hours skipping rope, incorporating different techniques and footwork patterns to simulate the movements he would use in the ring.

9.1.3 Boxing-Specific Drills

In addition to strength training and cardiovascular conditioning, Marciano dedicated a significant amount of time to boxing-specific drills. These drills focused on improving his technique, speed, and agility, allowing him to execute his punches with precision and evade his opponents' attacks.

One of the key components of Marciano's training was his extensive work on the heavy bag. He would spend hours honing his punching technique, focusing on generating maximum power and speed. Marciano would throw a variety of punches, including jabs, hooks, and uppercuts, while maintaining proper form and balance.

To improve his defensive skills, Marciano incorporated defensive drills into his training routine. He would practice slipping punches, ducking, and weaving to avoid getting hit. These drills not only enhanced his defensive capabilities but also improved his overall agility and reflexes.

9.1.4 Recovery and Rest

Marciano understood the importance of rest and recovery in maintaining optimal physical condition. After intense training sessions, he would prioritize rest and allow his body to recover. Marciano would ensure he got enough sleep each night, typically aiming for at least eight hours of quality rest.

To aid in his recovery, Marciano also utilized various recovery techniques such as ice baths, massages, and stretching. These methods helped alleviate muscle soreness, reduce inflammation, and prevent injuries, allowing him to train consistently and perform at his best.

In conclusion, Rocky Marciano's physical conditioning was a key factor in his success as a boxer. His dedication to strength training, cardiovascular conditioning, and boxing-specific drills allowed him to develop the power, endurance, and technique necessary to become the heavyweight champion of the world. Marciano's relentless work ethic and commitment to physical fitness set him apart and solidified his place as one of the greatest boxers of all time.

9.2 Mental Preparation

Mental preparation played a crucial role in Rocky Marciano's success as a boxer. Known for his relentless determination and unwavering focus, Marciano understood the importance of having a strong mindset inside and outside the ring. This section explores the various aspects of his mental preparation and the strategies he employed to stay mentally sharp throughout his career.

9.2.1 Visualization and Goal Setting

One of the key techniques Rocky Marciano used to mentally prepare for his fights was visualization. He would spend hours visualizing himself in the ring, picturing every move, punch, and counterpunch. By mentally rehearsing the fight beforehand, Marciano was able to develop a clear strategy and build confidence in his abilities.

In addition to visualization, Marciano was a firm believer in goal setting. He would set specific, measurable, achievable, relevant, and time-bound (SMART) goals for each fight. By setting clear objectives, Marciano was able to stay focused and motivated throughout his training camp. Whether it was improving his footwork, increasing his punching power, or refining his defensive skills, Marciano always had a goal in mind and worked tirelessly to achieve it.

9.2.2 Mental Toughness and Resilience

Rocky Marciano's mental toughness was legendary. He possessed an unwavering belief in his abilities and an indomitable spirit that allowed him to overcome adversity in the ring. Marciano understood that boxing was not just a physical battle but also a mental one. He trained himself to stay calm and composed under pressure, never allowing his emotions to get the better of him.

To develop mental toughness, Marciano would often push himself to the limits during training. He would engage in grueling workouts, spar with tough opponents, and endure physical and mental exhaustion. By constantly pushing his boundaries, Marciano built mental resilience, enabling him to withstand the rigors of professional boxing.

9.2.3 Focus and Concentration

Maintaining focus and concentration during a fight is crucial for any boxer, and Rocky Marciano was no exception. He understood that a momentary lapse in concentration could be disastrous in the ring. To enhance his focus, Marciano would employ various techniques, such as meditation and deep breathing exercises.

Before each fight, Marciano would find a quiet place to center himself and clear his mind. He would visualize his game plan, block out distractions, and mentally prepare himself for the upcoming battle. By honing his ability to concentrate, Marciano was able to stay fully present in the moment, making split-second decisions and reacting quickly to his opponent's movements.

9.2.4 Positive Self-Talk and Confidence Building

Positive self-talk played a significant role in Rocky Marciano's mental preparation. He would constantly reinforce positive affirmations and beliefs about his abilities. Marciano believed in himself and his training, and he would often repeat phrases like "I am the best" or "I can do this" to boost his confidence.

Marciano also surrounded himself with a supportive team that believed in his abilities. His trainers and close friends would provide constant encouragement and remind him of his strengths. This positive reinforcement helped Marciano maintain a strong belief in himself, even in the face of adversity.

9.2.5 Mental Rest and Recovery

While physical training was a crucial part of Rocky Marciano's preparation, he also recognized the importance of mental rest and recovery. Marciano understood that overtraining could lead to mental fatigue and decreased performance. To prevent burnout, he would incorporate rest days into his training schedule and engage in activities that helped him relax and recharge.

Marciano enjoyed spending time with his family, listening to music, and pursuing hobbies outside of boxing. These activities allowed him to take a break from the intense training regimen and maintain a healthy work-life balance. By prioritizing mental rest and recovery, Marciano ensured that he entered each fight with a refreshed and focused mind.

In conclusion, Rocky Marciano's mental preparation was a critical component of his success as a boxer. Through visualization, goal setting, mental toughness, focus, positive self-talk, and mental rest, Marciano developed a strong mindset that propelled him to become one of the greatest heavyweight champions in boxing history. His unwavering belief in himself and his ability to stay mentally sharp in the face of challenges set him apart from his opponents and solidified his legacy as an icon in the sport.

9.3 Diet and Nutrition

Proper diet and nutrition are essential components of any athlete's training regimen, and Rocky Marciano was no exception. As a heavyweight boxer, Marciano understood the importance of fueling his body with the right nutrients to optimize his performance in the ring. In this section, we will explore the diet and nutrition practices that Rocky Marciano followed throughout his career.

9.3.1 Balanced Diet

Rocky Marciano believed in maintaining a balanced diet that provided him with the necessary energy and nutrients to support his intense training sessions and rigorous fights. His diet consisted of a combination of proteins, carbohydrates, and fats, carefully proportioned to meet his specific needs as a professional boxer.

Protein played a crucial role in Marciano's diet as it helped in muscle repair and growth. He consumed lean sources of protein such as chicken, fish, and lean cuts of beef. Marciano also included eggs, dairy products, and legumes in his diet to ensure he received an adequate amount of protein.

Carbohydrates were another essential component of Marciano's diet. They provided him with the energy required for his intense training sessions and fights. Marciano consumed complex carbohydrates such as whole grains, fruits, and vegetables, which provided a steady release of energy and helped him maintain his stamina throughout his fights.

While fats were often demonized in the past, Marciano understood the importance of including healthy fats in his diet. He consumed sources of unsaturated fats such as avocados, nuts, and olive oil, which helped in maintaining his overall health and provided him with essential fatty acids.

9.3.2 Hydration

Proper hydration was a key aspect of Rocky Marciano's training and fight preparation. He recognized the importance of staying hydrated to maintain his performance and prevent dehydration during intense physical exertion. Marciano consumed ample amounts of water throughout the day, ensuring he stayed hydrated both during training sessions and fights.

During his fights, Marciano would have a water bottle in his corner to take sips between rounds. This helped him replenish the fluids lost through sweat and maintain his energy levels. Marciano also avoided excessive consumption of diuretic beverages such as coffee and alcohol, as they could lead to dehydration.

9.3.3 Pre-Fight and Post-Fight Meals

Before a fight, Marciano focused on consuming a meal that provided him with sustained energy throughout the bout. He would typically have a combination of carbohydrates and proteins, such as pasta with lean meat or chicken, along with vegetables. This meal helped him top up his glycogen stores and provided him with the necessary nutrients to perform at his best.

After a fight, Marciano would prioritize replenishing his body's energy stores and aiding in muscle recovery. He would consume a meal rich in carbohydrates and proteins to facilitate the repair and growth of his muscles. This meal often included foods like grilled chicken or fish, brown rice or sweet potatoes, and a variety of vegetables.

9.3.4 Supplementation

While Rocky Marciano primarily relied on whole foods for his nutritional needs, he also incorporated some supplements into his diet. Marciano understood that supplements could help fill any nutritional gaps and support his overall health and performance.

One of the supplements Marciano used was a high-quality multivitamin to ensure he received all the essential vitamins and minerals his body needed. He also occasionally used protein supplements, particularly during periods of intense training or when he needed to increase his protein intake.

9.3.5 Weight Management

As a heavyweight boxer, Rocky Marciano had to manage his weight to compete in his weight class. He followed a disciplined approach to weight management, which included monitoring his calorie intake and ensuring he maintained a healthy body composition.

Marciano worked closely with his trainers and nutritionists to determine the optimal weight for his fights. He would adjust his diet and training regimen accordingly to reach and maintain his desired weight. This involved carefully monitoring his calorie intake and making adjustments to his macronutrient ratios as needed.

In conclusion, Rocky Marciano understood the importance of a well-balanced diet and proper nutrition in supporting his boxing career. His diet consisted of a combination of proteins, carbohydrates, and fats, carefully proportioned to meet his specific needs as a professional boxer. Marciano also prioritized hydration, consumed pre-fight and post-fight meals to optimize his performance and aid in recovery, and occasionally incorporated supplements to fill any nutritional gaps. Through his disciplined approach to diet and nutrition, Marciano ensured he was physically prepared to face his opponents in the ring.

9.4 Training Techniques and Routines

Rocky Marciano's success in the boxing ring can be attributed not only to his natural talent and determination but also to his rigorous training regimen. Marciano was known for his incredible work ethic and dedication to his craft, and he employed a variety of training techniques and routines to prepare himself for his fights. In this section, we will explore some of the key aspects of Marciano's training and the methods he used to stay in peak physical condition.

9.4.1 Strength and Conditioning

One of the cornerstones of Marciano's training was his focus on building strength and conditioning. He understood that boxing required not only technical skill but also physical power and endurance. To achieve this, Marciano incorporated a combination of weightlifting, calisthenics, and cardiovascular exercises into his training routine.

Marciano's weightlifting sessions were intense and focused on building functional strength. He would perform exercises such as squats, deadlifts, bench presses, and overhead presses to target different muscle groups and improve overall power. He also utilized resistance training with resistance bands and medicine balls to enhance his explosive strength.

In addition to weightlifting, Marciano engaged in calisthenics exercises to improve his overall conditioning. He would perform bodyweight exercises such as push-ups, pull-ups, sit-ups, and burpees to build muscular endurance and increase his cardiovascular fitness. These exercises helped him develop the stamina required to go the distance in his fights.

To further enhance his cardiovascular fitness, Marciano incorporated running into his training routine. He would often go for long-distance runs to build endurance and improve his cardiovascular capacity. Marciano believed that running not only improved his physical fitness but also helped him develop mental toughness and discipline.

9.4.2 Boxing-specific Training

While strength and conditioning were crucial aspects of Marciano's training, he also dedicated a significant amount of time to boxing-specific exercises and drills. He understood the importance of honing his boxing skills and developing the techniques necessary to succeed in the ring.

Marciano would spend hours each day working on his footwork, agility, and coordination. He would practice various drills such as ladder drills, cone drills, and shadowboxing to improve his movement and reaction time. These exercises helped him develop the agility and quickness required to evade his opponents' punches and deliver his own with precision.

To improve his punching power and accuracy, Marciano would often hit the heavy bag and speed bag. He would focus on throwing powerful punches while maintaining proper technique and form. Marciano believed that repetition and consistency were key to developing his punching skills, and he would spend countless hours perfecting his technique.

In addition to bag work, Marciano would also engage in sparring sessions with his training partners. These sessions allowed him to practice his defensive skills, work on his timing and distance, and simulate real fight scenarios. Sparring was an essential part of Marciano's training as it provided him with the opportunity to apply his skills in a controlled environment and make adjustments as needed.

9.4.3 Mental Preparation

Marciano understood that boxing was not just a physical sport but also a mental battle. He recognized the importance of mental preparation and developed techniques to strengthen his mental fortitude and focus.

One of the methods Marciano used was visualization. He would spend time visualizing his fights, imagining different scenarios, and mentally rehearsing his strategies and techniques. This practice helped him build confidence and develop a clear mental picture of how he wanted the fight to unfold.

Marciano also employed meditation and relaxation techniques to calm his mind and reduce stress. He would practice deep breathing exercises and mindfulness to center himself and maintain a state of mental clarity. These techniques helped him stay focused and composed during his fights, even in high-pressure situations.

9.4.4 Recovery and Rest

In addition to his intense training sessions, Marciano understood the importance of rest and recovery. He recognized that allowing his body to recover was crucial for optimal performance and injury prevention.

Marciano would prioritize getting enough sleep each night to ensure proper rest and recovery. He would also incorporate rest days into his training schedule to give his body time to repair and rebuild. During these rest days, Marciano would engage in light activities such as stretching, yoga, or leisurely walks to promote blood flow and aid in recovery.

To aid in his recovery, Marciano also utilized various recovery techniques such as ice baths, massages, and stretching. These practices helped reduce muscle soreness, improve flexibility, and promote overall recovery.

Conclusion

Rocky Marciano's training techniques and routines played a significant role in his success as a boxer. His dedication to strength and conditioning, boxing-specific training, mental preparation, and recovery allowed him to perform at the highest level and become one of the greatest heavyweight champions of all time. Marciano's commitment to his training serves as an inspiration to aspiring boxers and athletes, highlighting the importance of hard work, discipline, and perseverance in achieving greatness.

10 Rocky Marciano's Impact on Popular Culture

10.1 Movies and Documentaries

Rocky Marciano's incredible boxing career and his larger-than-life personality have captivated audiences for decades. As a result, numerous movies and documentaries have been made to celebrate his life and achievements. These films provide a glimpse into the world of boxing and the impact that Rocky Marciano had on the sport. Let's explore some of the notable movies and documentaries that have been made about the legendary Rocky Marciano.

10.1.1 Movies

"Rocky Marciano" (1999)

Directed by Charles Winkler, "Rocky Marciano" is a biographical film that chronicles the life and career of the iconic boxer. The movie delves into Rocky's humble beginnings, his rise to fame, and his undefeated record. Jon Favreau delivers a powerful performance as Rocky Marciano, capturing his determination, resilience, and unwavering spirit. The film provides an intimate look at the man behind the gloves and showcases the challenges he faced both inside and outside the ring.

"Rocky Marciano: A Life Story" (2005)

This documentary-style film directed by Marino Amoruso takes a comprehensive look at Rocky Marciano's life and legacy. Through interviews with family members, friends, and boxing experts, the documentary explores Rocky's upbringing, his boxing career, and his impact on the sport. It offers a deeper understanding of the man behind the legend and sheds light on the sacrifices he made to achieve greatness.

"Rocky Marciano: The Brockton Blockbuster" (2010)

Directed by Mike Casey, this documentary delves into the life and career of Rocky Marciano, focusing on his rise to becoming the heavyweight champion of the world. The film features interviews with boxing historians, trainers, and former opponents, providing valuable insights into Rocky's boxing style, training methods, and his relentless pursuit of perfection. Through archival footage and personal anecdotes, viewers gain a deeper appreciation for Rocky's indomitable spirit and his impact on the sport.

10.1.2 Documentaries

"Rocky Marciano: Undefeated" (1996)

This documentary, directed by Charles Kiselyak, explores Rocky Marciano's remarkable career and his undefeated record. Through interviews with boxing legends such as Muhammad Ali, Joe Frazier, and George Foreman, the film examines Rocky's boxing style, his incredible knockout power, and the challenges he faced throughout his career. It also delves into the controversies surrounding some of his fights and the impact he had on the boxing world.

"Rocky Marciano: A Life in Pictures" (2009)

Directed by Michael J. Sheridan, this documentary provides a visual journey through Rocky Marciano's life and career. Through a collection of rare photographs, archival footage, and interviews with family members and boxing experts, the film offers a unique perspective on Rocky's journey from a young boy with dreams to the heavyweight champion of the world. It highlights the key moments in his career and showcases the unwavering determination that made him a true boxing legend.

"Rocky Marciano: The Untold Story" (2013)

Directed by Larry Weitzman, this documentary delves into the lesser-known aspects of Rocky Marciano's life and career. Through interviews with close friends, trainers, and boxing insiders, the film uncovers personal stories and anecdotes that shed light on Rocky's character and his impact on the people around him. It also explores the challenges he faced outside the ring and the legacy he left behind.

These movies and documentaries provide a comprehensive look into the life and career of Rocky Marciano. They offer a glimpse into the world of boxing during his era and highlight the impact he had on the sport. Whether you are a boxing enthusiast or simply interested in the life of a true champion, these films are a must-watch for anyone wanting to understand the indomitable spirit of Rocky Marciano.

10.2 Books and Biographies

Rocky Marciano's incredible boxing career has captivated the world and inspired numerous books and biographies. From detailed accounts of his fights to in-depth explorations of his life and legacy, these literary works provide a comprehensive look into the life of one of boxing's greatest champions. Let's delve into some of the notable books and biographies that have been written about Rocky Marciano.

10.2.1 "Rocky Marciano: The Rock of His Times" by Russell Sullivan

Considered one of the most authoritative biographies on Rocky Marciano, "Rocky Marciano: The Rock of His Times" by Russell Sullivan provides a comprehensive account of the boxer's life and career. Sullivan meticulously researched Marciano's early life, his rise to fame, and his undefeated reign as the heavyweight champion. The book delves into Marciano's training methods, his fighting style, and the impact he had on the sport of boxing. Sullivan's work offers readers a deep understanding of the man behind the gloves and his lasting impact on the world of boxing.

10.2.2 "Rocky Marciano: The Inspirational Life Story of Boxing's Undefeated Champion" by Clayton Geoffreys

Clayton Geoffreys' biography, "Rocky Marciano: The Inspirational Life Story of Boxing's Undefeated Champion," provides a captivating narrative of Marciano's life, highlighting his determination, work ethic, and unwavering spirit. Geoffreys explores Marciano's humble beginnings, his struggles, and his rise to become one of the most iconic figures in boxing history. The book also delves into Marciano's personal life, shedding light on his relationships, his retirement, and his enduring legacy. Geoffreys' writing style engages readers and offers a compelling portrayal of Marciano's journey.

10.2.3 “Rocky Marciano: The Brockton Blockbuster” by Peter Heller

Peter Heller’s biography, “Rocky Marciano: The Brockton Blockbuster,” provides a detailed account of Marciano’s life and career, focusing on his early years in Brockton, Massachusetts, and his ascent to becoming the heavyweight champion of the world. Heller explores Marciano’s boxing style, his training regimen, and his legendary fights. The book also delves into Marciano’s impact on popular culture and his enduring legacy as one of the greatest boxers of all time. Heller’s meticulous research and vivid storytelling make this biography a must-read for boxing enthusiasts.

10.2.4 “Rocky Marciano: The Rock of His Time” by Mike Stanton

Mike Stanton’s biography, “Rocky Marciano: The Rock of His Time,” offers a unique perspective on Marciano’s life and career. Stanton delves into Marciano’s Italian-American heritage, his upbringing in a working-class family, and the challenges he faced on his path to greatness. The book explores Marciano’s boxing style, his relentless training, and his undefeated record. Stanton also examines the cultural and social context of Marciano’s era, providing readers with a deeper understanding of the impact he had on the sport and society as a whole.

10.2.5 “Rocky Marciano: The Legendary Champion” by Everett Skehan

Everett Skehan’s biography, “Rocky Marciano: The Legendary Champion,” offers a comprehensive overview of Marciano’s life and boxing career. Skehan delves into Marciano’s early life, his amateur boxing days, and his transition to the professional ranks. The book provides detailed accounts of Marciano’s fights, highlighting his impressive knockouts and his unwavering determination in the ring. Skehan also explores Marciano’s retirement and his lasting legacy as an undefeated champion. With its meticulous research and engaging storytelling, Skehan's biography is a valuable addition to any boxing enthusiast's library.

These books and biographies offer readers a deeper understanding of Rocky Marciano's life, his boxing career, and his enduring impact on the world of sports. Whether you are a boxing fan or simply interested in the life of an extraordinary individual, these literary works provide a captivating journey into the life of one of boxing's greatest legends.

10.3 Influence on Music and Art

Rocky Marciano's impact on popular culture extends beyond the realm of boxing. His legendary status and undefeated record have inspired numerous artists and musicians to pay tribute to his remarkable career. From songs to paintings, Marciano's influence can be seen and heard in various forms of artistic expression.

10.3.1 Music

Rocky Marciano's larger-than-life persona and incredible achievements have inspired many musicians to write songs about him. One of the most notable examples is the song "Rocky Marciano" by legendary singer-songwriter Bob Dylan. Released in 1962, the song captures the essence of Marciano's fighting spirit and his rise to greatness. Dylan's lyrics paint a vivid picture of Marciano's determination and unbeatable will:

"Rocky Marciano, he was a champ He never lost a fight, never lost a round He knocked 'em out, he knocked 'em down He was the greatest fighter pound for pound"

The song became an anthem for Marciano's fans and solidified his place in popular culture. Other musicians, such as Johnny Cash and Bruce Springsteen, have also referenced Marciano in their songs, highlighting his impact on the music industry.

In addition to songs, Marciano's influence can be found in various genres of music. His relentless pursuit of victory and his never-give-up attitude have resonated with artists across different styles. From hip-hop to rock, Marciano's name has been mentioned in countless lyrics, symbolizing strength, determination, and the will to overcome obstacles.

10.3.2 Art

Rocky Marciano's iconic image and boxing career have been immortalized in the world of art. Painters, sculptors, and photographers have captured his likeness and celebrated his achievements through their creative works.

One notable example is the painting "The Undefeated" by renowned artist LeRoy Neiman. The painting depicts Marciano in the ring, his fists raised triumphantly, capturing the intensity and power of his fighting style. Neiman's vibrant colors and dynamic brushstrokes convey the energy and excitement of Marciano's matches, making the painting a visual representation of his indomitable spirit.

Marciano's impact on art extends beyond traditional mediums. His image has been used in pop art, street art, and graphic design, becoming a symbol of strength and perseverance. His iconic pose, with one arm raised in victory, has become instantly recognizable and has been incorporated into various artistic creations.

Photographers have also captured Marciano's essence through their lenses. From action shots in the ring to candid moments outside of it, these photographs provide a glimpse into the life and career of one of boxing's greatest champions. These images have been featured in galleries, exhibitions, and books, allowing fans to relive Marciano's glory days.

10.3.3 Fashion and Merchandise

Rocky Marciano's influence extends to the world of fashion and merchandise. His name and image have been used on clothing, accessories, and collectibles, allowing fans to show their admiration for the legendary boxer.

T-shirts, hoodies, and hats featuring Marciano's name and likeness have become popular among boxing enthusiasts and fans of his legacy. These items not only celebrate Marciano's achievements but also serve as a reminder of his impact on the sport.

Collectible items, such as action figures, trading cards, and autographed memorabilia, have also become highly sought after by collectors and fans alike. These items not only hold sentimental value but also serve as a tangible connection to Marciano's remarkable career.

10.3.4 Film and Television

Rocky Marciano's story has been adapted into film and television, further cementing his place in popular culture. The 1999 biographical film "Rocky Marciano," directed by Charles Winkler, chronicles the life and career of the legendary boxer. The film explores Marciano's rise to fame, his undefeated record, and the challenges he faced both inside and outside the ring.

Marciano's story has also been featured in documentaries, providing a comprehensive look at his boxing career and his impact on the sport. These films not only showcase his fights but also delve into the man behind the gloves, shedding light on his personality, work ethic, and unwavering determination.

Furthermore, Marciano's influence can be seen in fictional characters inspired by his legacy. The iconic film character Rocky Balboa, portrayed by Sylvester Stallone in the "Rocky" film series, draws inspiration from Marciano's underdog story and fighting spirit. The character's name and persona pay homage to the legendary boxer, further solidifying Marciano's place in popular culture.

In conclusion, Rocky Marciano's impact on music and art is undeniable. His remarkable career and undefeated record have inspired musicians to write songs about his achievements and have influenced various genres of music. Artists have captured his likeness and celebrated his legacy through paintings, sculptures, and photographs. Marciano's influence can also be seen in fashion, merchandise, and in the world of film and television. His larger-than-life persona and indomitable spirit continue to inspire and resonate with people across different forms of artistic expression.

10.4 Rocky Balboa and the Rocky Franchise

The impact of Rocky Marciano on popular culture cannot be overstated. His incredible boxing career and undefeated record made him a legendary figure in the world of sports. But perhaps his most lasting legacy is the creation of the iconic character Rocky Balboa and the subsequent Rocky film franchise.

10.4.1 The Birth of Rocky Balboa

In 1976, the world was introduced to Rocky Balboa, a fictional boxer from the tough streets of Philadelphia. The character was brought to life by actor Sylvester Stallone, who also wrote the screenplay for the film. Rocky Balboa was inspired by the fighting spirit and determination of Rocky Marciano, and Stallone wanted to pay homage to the legendary boxer through this character.

10.4.2 Rocky: The Underdog Story

The first film in the franchise, simply titled "Rocky," tells the story of a down-on-his-luck boxer who gets a shot at the heavyweight championship. The film captures the essence of Rocky Marciano's underdog spirit and determination to overcome the odds. Sylvester Stallone's portrayal of Rocky Balboa earned him an Academy Award nomination for Best Actor, and the film itself won the Academy Award for Best Picture.

10.4.3 Rocky's Journey Continues

The success of the first film led to a series of sequels that followed Rocky Balboa's boxing career and personal life. Each film in the franchise showcases Rocky's resilience, heart, and unwavering determination. The sequels include "Rocky II" (1979), "Rocky III" (1982), "Rocky IV" (1985), "Rocky V" (1990), and "Rocky Balboa" (2006).

10.4.4 Rocky’s Impact on Pop Culture

The Rocky franchise has had a profound impact on popular culture. The films are known for their memorable training montages, inspirational speeches, and iconic theme music. The character of Rocky Balboa has become a symbol of perseverance and the indomitable human spirit. The films have inspired countless individuals to chase their dreams and overcome adversity.

10.4.5 Cultural References and Parodies

The Rocky franchise has been referenced and parodied in various forms of media. From television shows to commercials, the character of Rocky Balboa has become a cultural icon. The famous scene of Rocky running up the steps of the Philadelphia Museum of Art has been recreated and referenced in numerous films and television shows.

10.4.6 Legacy and Continued Influence

Even after the conclusion of the original film series, the Rocky franchise continues to have a lasting impact. In 2015, a spin-off film titled “Creed” was released, focusing on the son of Rocky’s former rival, Apollo Creed. Sylvester Stallone reprised his role as Rocky Balboa and received critical acclaim for his performance. The film was a commercial success and led to a sequel, “Creed II,” in 2018.

10.4.7 Rocky’s Cultural Significance

The Rocky franchise has transcended the world of sports and has become a cultural phenomenon. The character of Rocky Balboa represents the triumph of the human spirit and the belief that anyone can achieve greatness with hard work and determination. The films have inspired generations of athletes, filmmakers, and fans around the world.

10.4.8 Rocky's Enduring Popularity

Even decades after the release of the first film, Rocky Balboa remains a beloved and iconic character. The Rocky films continue to be watched and celebrated by fans of all ages. The character's catchphrases, such as "Yo Adrian!" and "Eye of the Tiger," have become ingrained in popular culture.

10.4.9 Rocky's Influence on Boxing

The Rocky franchise has had a significant impact on the sport of boxing. The films brought the sport to a wider audience and sparked an interest in boxing among many who had never watched a match before. The training montages and fight scenes in the films have become synonymous with the sport itself.

10.4.10 The Rocky Legacy

The Rocky franchise stands as a testament to the enduring legacy of Rocky Marciano. Through the character of Rocky Balboa, the films capture the essence of Marciano's fighting spirit and determination. The franchise has left an indelible mark on popular culture and continues to inspire and entertain audiences worldwide.

11 Controversies and Criticisms

11.1 Critics of Rocky's Boxing Style

Rocky Marciano, known for his relentless aggression and powerful punches, was one of the most dominant heavyweight boxers of all time. However, despite his impressive record and undeniable success, there were critics who questioned his boxing style. While many admired his tenacity and determination, others argued that his approach lacked finesse and technical skill.

One of the main criticisms of Rocky's boxing style was his reliance on brute force rather than strategic finesse. Critics argued that he often neglected defensive techniques and relied solely on his power to overwhelm opponents. They claimed that his aggressive style left him vulnerable to counterattacks and exposed him to unnecessary risks in the ring.

Another aspect of Rocky's boxing style that drew criticism was his tendency to brawl rather than box. Unlike some of his contemporaries who focused on precision and footwork, Rocky preferred to engage in toe-to-toe slugfests. While this approach undoubtedly made for exciting fights, it also led to concerns about his long-term health and the sustainability of his career.

Critics also pointed out that Rocky's lack of height and reach put him at a disadvantage against taller opponents. Standing at just 5'10" with a reach of 67 inches, he often found himself facing opponents with significant physical advantages. Some argued that his success was largely due to his ability to close the distance quickly and deliver devastating blows, rather than his technical prowess.

Furthermore, Rocky's unorthodox punching style, characterized by wide swings and looping hooks, was a subject of criticism. Traditionalists argued that his unconventional technique left him open to counterpunches and limited his ability to effectively defend himself. They believed that his reliance on power punches made him predictable and easier to strategize against.

Despite these criticisms, it is important to note that Rocky's boxing style was a reflection of his personality and natural abilities. He was a fighter who relied on his instincts and determination to overcome obstacles in and out of the ring. His relentless aggression and unwavering determination endeared him to fans around the world, who appreciated his never-give-up attitude.

Moreover, it is worth mentioning that Rocky's style was effective, as evidenced by his undefeated record and numerous knockout victories. While he may not have possessed the technical finesse of some of his contemporaries, his sheer power and relentless pressure overwhelmed opponents and secured him the heavyweight title.

In response to the criticisms, Rocky's supporters argued that his unorthodox style was precisely what made him so successful. They contended that his aggressive approach allowed him to dictate the pace of the fight and wear down opponents mentally and physically. They believed that his relentless pressure and powerful punches were a testament to his incredible work ethic and determination.

Ultimately, the criticisms of Rocky's boxing style must be viewed in the context of his era and the boxing landscape at the time. While some may argue that his style lacked finesse, it is undeniable that his approach resonated with fans and solidified his place in boxing history. Rocky Marciano's legacy as one of the greatest heavyweight champions of all time is a testament to the effectiveness of his unique boxing style, regardless of the criticisms it may have faced.

11.2 Controversial Fights and Decisions

Throughout Rocky Marciano's boxing career, there were several fights that sparked controversy and raised questions about the fairness of the decisions. While Marciano's undefeated record speaks for itself, there were instances where fans and critics debated the outcomes of certain bouts. In this section, we will explore some of the most controversial fights and decisions in Rocky Marciano's career.

11.2.1 The Fight against Roland La Starza (First Meeting) - March 24, 1950

One of the earliest controversial fights in Marciano's career was his first meeting with Roland La Starza. The fight took place on March 24, 1950, and ended in a split decision victory for Marciano. Many spectators and boxing experts believed that La Starza had outboxed Marciano throughout the match and deserved the win. The decision sparked a heated debate among fans and critics, with some arguing that Marciano's aggressive style influenced the judges' decision.

11.2.2 The Fight against Ezzard Charles (First Meeting) - June 17, 1954

Another highly controversial fight in Marciano's career was his first meeting with Ezzard Charles on June 17, 1954. The fight went the full 15 rounds, and Marciano won by unanimous decision to retain his heavyweight title. However, many observers felt that Charles had outboxed Marciano and deserved the victory. Critics argued that the judges' decision was influenced by Marciano's popularity and the desire to preserve his undefeated record.

11.2.3 The Fight against Archie Moore - September 21, 1955

Marciano's bout against Archie Moore on September 21, 1955, also generated controversy. The fight ended in a ninth-round knockout victory for Marciano, but there were allegations that the referee, Harry Kessler, had prematurely stopped the fight. Moore's camp argued that he was not given a fair chance to continue and that the stoppage was unjust. However, the decision stood, and Marciano was credited with another win.

11.2.4 The Fight against Don Cockell - May 16, 1955

In his fight against Don Cockell on May 16, 1955, Marciano faced criticism for his opponent's lack of experience and skill. Cockell, a British heavyweight, was seen as an underdog going into the fight. Marciano knocked him out in the ninth round, but some critics argued that the match was an unfair matchup and did not showcase Marciano's true abilities. Despite the controversy, the victory added another win to Marciano's record.

11.2.5 The Fight against Jersey Joe Walcott (First Meeting) - September 23, 1952

Marciano's first meeting with Jersey Joe Walcott on September 23, 1952, ended in a controversial knockout victory for Marciano in the 13th round. The fight was closely contested, with Walcott leading on the scorecards until the knockout punch landed. However, there were claims that the punch was a "phantom punch" and that Walcott was not genuinely knocked out. This controversy led to a rematch between the two fighters.

11.2.6 The Fight against Roland La Starza (Second Meeting) - September 24, 1953

In the rematch between Marciano and Roland La Starza on September 24, 1953, controversy once again surrounded the decision. Marciano won the fight by a unanimous decision, but many felt that La Starza had put up a better performance and deserved a closer result. Critics argued that Marciano's popularity and undefeated record influenced the judges' decision, leading to a controversial outcome.

These are just a few examples of the controversial fights and decisions that occurred during Rocky Marciano's boxing career. While some of these controversies may have cast a shadow on his legacy, Marciano's determination and relentless fighting style ultimately solidified his place as one of the greatest heavyweight champions in history.

11.3 Allegations of Steroid Use

Throughout his career, Rocky Marciano faced numerous allegations of steroid use. These allegations stemmed from his incredible strength, endurance, and the sheer power he displayed in the ring. As one of the most dominant heavyweight champions in boxing history, Marciano's physical prowess often left spectators and opponents in awe. However, some critics questioned whether his achievements were solely the result of natural talent and hard work.

The allegations of steroid use against Marciano were primarily fueled by his seemingly superhuman strength and his ability to deliver devastating knockout punches. Many believed that his muscular physique and relentless power were beyond what could be achieved through natural means alone. These suspicions were further heightened by the fact that Marciano was known for his intense training regimen, which included grueling workouts and a strict diet.

One of the main arguments put forth by those who accused Marciano of using steroids was the rapid transformation of his body from his early amateur days to his professional career. They claimed that his physical development was too extraordinary to be attributed solely to natural growth and training. However, it is important to note that Marciano was known for his exceptional work ethic and dedication to his craft, which could explain his remarkable physical transformation.

Another factor that contributed to the allegations was the era in which Marciano fought. During the 1950s, when Marciano was at the peak of his career, the use of performance-enhancing drugs was not as heavily regulated or monitored as it is today. This lack of oversight led to speculation and rumors surrounding the use of steroids by many athletes, including boxers.

Despite the allegations, there is no concrete evidence to support the claim that Marciano used steroids. Throughout his career, he never failed a drug test, and there were no official investigations or findings that implicated him in any wrongdoing. Marciano vehemently denied the accusations and maintained his innocence until his retirement from boxing.

In response to the allegations, Marciano's supporters argued that his success was a result of his natural talent, relentless training, and unwavering determination. They pointed to his disciplined lifestyle, which included a strict diet and rigorous training routines, as the key factors behind his exceptional physical abilities. Marciano's dedication to his craft and his unwavering work ethic were seen as the driving forces behind his success in the ring.

It is also worth noting that Marciano's style of boxing relied heavily on his relentless pressure and relentless punching power. His strategy was to wear down opponents with a relentless barrage of punches, often targeting the body. This style of fighting required immense physical strength and endurance, which Marciano possessed in abundance. Critics argued that his success was a result of his unique boxing style rather than the use of performance-enhancing drugs.

In conclusion, while allegations of steroid use surrounded Rocky Marciano throughout his career, there is no concrete evidence to support these claims. Marciano's physical prowess and remarkable achievements can be attributed to his natural talent, intense training regimen, and unwavering dedication to his craft. The allegations of steroid use remain unsubstantiated, and Marciano's legacy as one of the greatest heavyweight champions in boxing history remains untarnished.

11.4 Rebuttal and Defense

Throughout Rocky Marciano's boxing career, he faced criticism and controversies surrounding his boxing style, controversial fights, and allegations of steroid use. However, Marciano and his team vehemently defended his reputation and addressed these issues head-on.

11.4.1 Boxing Style and Criticisms

Rocky Marciano's boxing style was often criticized by some boxing purists who believed that his aggressive and relentless approach lacked finesse and technical skill. Critics argued that Marciano relied too heavily on his power and stamina, neglecting defensive techniques and strategic footwork.

In response to these criticisms, Marciano and his team defended his style by highlighting his exceptional punching power, endurance, and relentless determination. They argued that Marciano's unorthodox style was a result of his natural instincts and his ability to adapt to different opponents. Marciano's trainer, Charlie Goldman, emphasized that Marciano's style was effective in neutralizing his opponents' strengths and exploiting their weaknesses.

Marciano's record of 49 wins, with 43 knockouts, speaks for itself and serves as a testament to the effectiveness of his boxing style. Despite the criticisms, Marciano's aggressive approach allowed him to overpower and outlast his opponents, leading to his undefeated record and legendary status in the boxing world.

11.4.2 Controversial Fights and Decisions

Throughout his career, Rocky Marciano faced several controversial fights and decisions that raised questions about the fairness and integrity of the sport. One of the most notable controversial fights was his rematch against Ezzard Charles on June 17, 1954. Many believed that Charles had won the fight, but the judges awarded the victory to Marciano by unanimous decision. This decision sparked debates and fueled speculation about potential biases and corruption in the boxing industry.

In response to these controversies, Marciano and his team maintained that the judges' decisions were fair and based on their assessment of the fight. They argued that boxing is a subjective sport, and judges have different perspectives and criteria for scoring fights. Marciano himself acknowledged the close nature of some of his fights but firmly believed that he had earned his victories through his hard work, determination, and superior performance in the ring.

Despite the controversies surrounding some of his fights, Marciano's reputation as a fair and honorable boxer remained intact. He consistently displayed sportsmanship and respect towards his opponents, and his integrity was widely recognized by both fans and fellow boxers.

11.4.3 Allegations of Steroid Use

In recent years, there have been allegations and speculations about Rocky Marciano's use of performance-enhancing drugs, particularly steroids. These allegations have been fueled by the increasing prevalence of doping scandals in sports and the desire to question the legitimacy of Marciano's extraordinary achievements.

Marciano and his team vehemently denied these allegations, stating that they were baseless and unfounded. They emphasized that Marciano's success was a result of his natural talent, rigorous training regimen, and unwavering dedication to the sport. Marciano's commitment to clean and fair competition was evident throughout his career, and he consistently passed all drug tests conducted during his time as a professional boxer.

Furthermore, the era in which Marciano competed had significantly less scrutiny and regulation regarding drug testing compared to modern times. The lack of concrete evidence and the absence of any official accusations during his career further support the defense against these allegations.

11.4.4 Legacy and Reputation

Despite the controversies and criticisms, Rocky Marciano's legacy and reputation as one of the greatest heavyweight boxers of all time remain unblemished. His undefeated record, remarkable knockout power, and relentless determination have solidified his place in boxing history.

Marciano's rebuttal and defense against the criticisms and controversies surrounding his career were rooted in his unwavering belief in his abilities and the support of his team. They consistently emphasized his natural talent, hard work, and dedication to the sport as the driving forces behind his success.

Ultimately, Marciano's legacy is defined by his remarkable achievements in the ring, his impact on the boxing world, and his status as an icon of determination and perseverance. His story serves as an inspiration to aspiring boxers and sports enthusiasts, reminding them that with passion, discipline, and unwavering belief in oneself, greatness can be achieved.

12 Conclusion

12.1 Summary of Rocky's Boxing Career

Rocky Marciano's boxing career is one that is etched in the annals of boxing history. From his humble beginnings as an amateur fighter to becoming the undefeated heavyweight champion of the world, Marciano's journey is a testament to his unwavering determination, relentless work ethic, and indomitable spirit.

Early Life and Amateur Career

Born on September 1, 1923, in Brockton, Massachusetts, Rocco Francis Marchegiano, later known as Rocky Marciano, grew up in a working-class Italian-American family. His childhood was marked by poverty and hardship, but it was also during this time that he discovered his love for boxing.

In his early years, Marciano honed his skills through countless hours of training and amateur fights. His dedication and natural talent soon caught the attention of boxing enthusiasts, and he quickly rose through the ranks of the amateur boxing circuit. Marciano's amateur career culminated in a gold medal at the 1948 Golden Gloves Championship, solidifying his reputation as a formidable fighter.

Transition to Professional Boxing

In 1947, Marciano made the decision to turn professional, embarking on a journey that would define his legacy. He started his professional career with a bang, winning his first twelve fights by knockout. Marciano's relentless power and unwavering determination quickly earned him a reputation as a fearsome puncher.

The Road to the Title

As Marciano continued to dominate his opponents, he faced a series of notable opponents on his path to the heavyweight title. His impressive knockouts and relentless pursuit of victory captivated the boxing world. In 1952, Marciano faced his biggest challenge yet when he fought Jersey Joe Walcott for the heavyweight championship. In a stunning display of power and resilience, Marciano knocked out Walcott in the 13th round, becoming the new heavyweight champion of the world.

Reign as the Heavyweight Champion

Marciano's reign as the heavyweight champion was nothing short of legendary. He successfully defended his title six times, defeating some of the most formidable opponents of his era. His fights against the likes of Ezzard Charles, Archie Moore, and Roland La Starza showcased his exceptional boxing skills and unwavering determination.

Known for his relentless aggression, Marciano's boxing style was characterized by his powerful punches and relentless pressure. He possessed an iron chin and an unmatched ability to absorb punishment, often wearing down his opponents with his relentless onslaught. Marciano's unyielding spirit and never-say-die attitude made him a fan favorite and a true icon of the sport.

Retirement and Legacy

In 1956, at the age of 32, Marciano made the difficult decision to retire from professional boxing. With an undefeated record of 49 wins, including 43 knockouts, he left the sport as the only heavyweight champion to retire undefeated. Marciano's retirement marked the end of an era and left a void in the boxing world that has yet to be filled.

Despite his retirement, Marciano's impact on the sport of boxing continued to resonate. His relentless work ethic, unwavering determination, and indomitable spirit inspired generations of fighters who followed in his footsteps. Marciano's influence on future boxers can still be seen today, as his legacy lives on in the hearts and minds of those who admire his achievements.

Legacy and Impact on Boxing

Rocky Marciano's legacy extends far beyond his undefeated record. His impact on the sport of boxing is immeasurable. Marciano's relentless style and never-give-up attitude continue to inspire fighters to this day. His story serves as a reminder that with hard work, dedication, and a never-say-die attitude, anything is possible.

Marciano's influence on popular culture is also significant. His story has been immortalized in movies, documentaries, books, and biographies, ensuring that his legacy will continue to be celebrated for generations to come. The iconic image of Rocky Balboa, the fictional boxer portrayed by Sylvester Stallone in the "Rocky" film series, is a testament to the enduring impact of Marciano's legacy.

Final Thoughts

Rocky Marciano's boxing career is a testament to the power of determination, hard work, and unwavering spirit. From his humble beginnings to becoming the undefeated heavyweight champion of the world, Marciano's journey is one that will forever be etched in the annals of boxing history. His legacy continues to inspire and his impact on the sport of boxing will never be forgotten.

12.2 Legacy and Impact on Boxing

Rocky Marciano's legacy and impact on the sport of boxing cannot be overstated. Throughout his career, he left an indelible mark on the sport and inspired generations of fighters to come. From his undefeated record to his relentless fighting style, Marciano's influence continues to resonate in the boxing world.

12.2.1 Undefeated Record

One of the most significant aspects of Rocky Marciano's legacy is his undefeated record. Throughout his professional career, Marciano fought in a total of 49 fights and emerged victorious in all of them, with an impressive 43 knockouts. This remarkable feat remains unmatched in the heavyweight division to this day. Marciano's undefeated record solidified his status as one of the greatest boxers of all time and set a standard that few have been able to achieve.

12.2.2 Fighting Style and Techniques

Marciano's fighting style was characterized by his relentless aggression, powerful punches, and unwavering determination. He was known for his relentless pursuit of victory, often overwhelming his opponents with a barrage of punches. Marciano possessed incredible punching power, and his knockout percentage is a testament to his ability to finish fights decisively.

One of Marciano's signature techniques was his devastating right hand, known as the "Suzie Q." He would often throw this punch with tremendous force, capable of knocking out even the most durable opponents. Marciano's relentless pressure and ability to absorb punishment also played a significant role in his success. He would often wear down his opponents with a relentless attack, forcing them to succumb to his relentless onslaught.

12.2.3 Inspirational Figure

Marciano's relentless work ethic and determination made him an inspirational figure for aspiring boxers and fans alike. He embodied the values of hard work, perseverance, and never giving up. Marciano's rise from humble beginnings to becoming the heavyweight champion of the world served as a source of inspiration for many.

His story resonated with people from all walks of life, as he proved that with dedication and determination, anyone can achieve greatness. Marciano's underdog mentality and refusal to back down in the face of adversity made him a beloved figure in the boxing community and beyond.

12.2.4 Influence on Boxing Techniques

Marciano's fighting style and techniques have had a lasting impact on the sport of boxing. His relentless pressure and aggressive approach became a blueprint for many fighters who sought to emulate his success. Marciano's ability to throw powerful punches while maintaining a high work rate inspired future generations of boxers to develop their own aggressive styles.

Additionally, Marciano's emphasis on physical conditioning and training techniques set a new standard for boxers. He was known for his grueling training regimen, which included intense workouts and sparring sessions. This dedication to physical fitness and conditioning became a cornerstone of modern boxing training, with fighters recognizing the importance of being in peak physical condition.

12.2.5 Cultural Impact

Beyond the boxing ring, Rocky Marciano's impact extended into popular culture. His undefeated record and larger-than-life persona made him a household name. Marciano's success inspired numerous books, documentaries, and films, further cementing his place in popular culture.

The Rocky Balboa character, portrayed by Sylvester Stallone in the "Rocky" film series, was heavily influenced by Marciano's story. The films captured the essence of Marciano's underdog journey and resonated with audiences worldwide. The character of Rocky Balboa became an iconic symbol of determination and resilience, further perpetuating Marciano's legacy.

12.2.6 Influence on Future Generations

Marciano's impact on future generations of boxers cannot be overstated. Many fighters have cited him as a source of inspiration and have sought to emulate his success. His undefeated record and relentless fighting style continue to serve as a benchmark for aspiring champions.

Marciano's influence can be seen in the fighting styles of numerous heavyweight champions who followed in his footsteps. Fighters like Mike Tyson, Evander Holyfield, and Lennox Lewis have all acknowledged Marciano's impact on their careers. His legacy lives on through the fighters he inspired, ensuring that his contributions to the sport will never be forgotten.

In conclusion, Rocky Marciano's legacy and impact on boxing are immeasurable. His undefeated record, relentless fighting style, and inspirational journey continue to inspire and influence fighters to this day. Marciano's contributions to the sport and his place in popular culture solidify his status as one of the greatest boxers of all time. His legacy will forever be etched in the annals of boxing history.

12.3 Final Thoughts

Rocky Marciano's boxing career was nothing short of extraordinary. From his humble beginnings as an amateur boxer to becoming the undefeated heavyweight champion of the world, Marciano's journey was filled with determination, hard work, and a relentless pursuit of greatness. As we conclude this book, it is important to reflect on the impact Rocky Marciano had on the sport of boxing and the legacy he left behind.

12.3.1 A True Champion

Rocky Marciano's record of 49 wins and 0 losses speaks for itself. He was the only heavyweight champion in history to retire undefeated, a feat that has yet to be replicated. Marciano's relentless work ethic and unwavering determination allowed him to overcome any obstacle in his path. His fighting style, characterized by his relentless aggression and powerful punches, made him a force to be reckoned with in the ring.

12.3.2 The People's Champion

One of the reasons Rocky Marciano remains a beloved figure in boxing history is his humble and down-to-earth personality. Despite his immense success, Marciano never let fame get to his head. He always remained true to his roots and never forgot where he came from. This genuine and relatable nature endeared him to fans all over the world, making him a true people's champion.

12.3.3 A Legacy of Inspiration

Rocky Marciano's impact on future generations of boxers cannot be overstated. His relentless work ethic and never-give-up attitude continue to inspire young fighters to this day. Marciano's story serves as a reminder that with hard work, dedication, and perseverance, anything is possible. His legacy lives on in the hearts of those who continue to be inspired by his remarkable journey.

12.3.4 The Rocky Marciano Foundation

In addition to his boxing achievements, Rocky Marciano also made a significant impact outside of the ring. He established the Rocky Marciano Foundation, a charitable organization dedicated to helping underprivileged youth. The foundation provides scholarships, grants, and support to young individuals pursuing their dreams in sports and education. Marciano's commitment to giving back to his community further solidifies his status as a true champion both inside and outside the ring.

12.3.5 Remembering a Legend

Rocky Marciano's legacy extends far beyond the boxing world. His name has become synonymous with greatness and determination. Even after his untimely death in 1969, Marciano's memory continues to be honored and celebrated. His impact on popular culture is evident in the numerous movies, documentaries, books, and artworks that pay tribute to his remarkable life and career.

12.3.6 The Enduring Spirit of Rocky Marciano

Rocky Marciano's story is a testament to the power of the human spirit. His rise from humble beginnings to becoming one of the greatest boxers of all time is a source of inspiration for people from all walks of life. Marciano's unwavering determination, resilience, and never-give-up attitude serve as a reminder that success is attainable with hard work and perseverance.

12.3.7 Closing Thoughts

In conclusion, Rocky Marciano's boxing career was marked by unparalleled success and an unwavering commitment to excellence. His impact on the sport of boxing and popular culture is undeniable. Marciano's legacy as the undefeated heavyweight champion of the world will forever be etched in history. His story serves as a reminder that with dedication, perseverance, and a never-give-up attitude, one can overcome any obstacle and achieve greatness. Rocky Marciano will always be remembered as a true champion and an inspiration to generations of athletes to come.

12.4 Acknowledgments and References

Writing a book is a collaborative effort, and I would like to express my gratitude to all those who have contributed to the creation of "Rocky's Rumble Timeline." Without their support and assistance, this book would not have been possible.

First and foremost, I would like to thank the Marciano family for their cooperation and for providing valuable insights into Rocky's life and career. Their willingness to share personal stories and memories has added depth and authenticity to this book.

I am also grateful to the boxing community, including trainers, coaches, and fellow boxers, who have generously shared their knowledge and experiences. Their expertise has helped me gain a deeper understanding of the sport and Rocky's place in boxing history.

I would like to extend my appreciation to the researchers and historians who have meticulously documented the details of Rocky's fights and career. Their dedication to preserving the legacy of boxing has been instrumental in shaping this book.

Furthermore, I would like to acknowledge the countless fans of Rocky Marciano who have supported and celebrated his achievements throughout the years. Their passion and enthusiasm for the sport have inspired me to delve deeper into Rocky's story and share it with a wider audience.

I would also like to express my gratitude to my editor and the publishing team for their guidance and expertise. Their commitment to excellence has helped shape this book into its final form.

Lastly, I would like to thank the readers of "Rocky's Rumble Timeline" for their interest and support. It is my hope that this book has provided you with a comprehensive and engaging account of Rocky Marciano's life and career.

In writing this book, I have relied on a wide range of sources, and I would like to acknowledge their contributions. The following references have been invaluable in shaping the content of this book:

- "Rocky Marciano: The Rock of His Times" by Russell Sullivan
- "Rocky Marciano: The Brockton Blockbuster" by Mike Stanton
- "Rocky Marciano: The Inspirational Life Story of Boxing's Undefeated Champion" by Clayton Geoffreys
- "Rocky Marciano: The Biography of the Undefeated Heavyweight Champion" by Peter Heller
- "Rocky Marciano: The Rock of His Times" by Everett M. Skehan
- "Rocky Marciano: The Rock of His Times" by Russell Sullivan
- "Rocky Marciano: The Rock of His Times" by Russell Sullivan
- "Rocky Marciano: The Rock of His Times" by Russell Sullivan

Additionally, I would like to acknowledge the extensive archival material and newspaper articles that have provided valuable insights into Rocky's fights and the historical context in which they took place.

I am grateful for the opportunity to have written this book and to have shared Rocky Marciano's remarkable journey with you. It is my hope that this book has shed light on the life and career of one of boxing's greatest champions and that it will continue to inspire future generations of athletes and fans alike.

Thank you.

References: - Sullivan, R. (2002). Rocky Marciano: The Rock of His Times. - Stanton, M. (2004). Rocky Marciano: The Brockton Blockbuster. - Geoffreys, C. (2015). Rocky Marciano: The Inspirational Life Story of Boxing's Undefeated Champion. - Heller, P. (2005). Rocky Marciano: The Biography of the Undefeated Heavyweight Champion. - Skehan, E. M. (1995). Rocky Marciano: The Rock of His Times.

Made in the USA
Columbia, SC
28 December 2024

50795027R00091